Dedicated to my mom and dad, Archana and Sudhakar Borle. To have faith in myself despite my ups and downs.

Contents

FROM LOCAL TO GLOBAL: THE ULTIMATE GUIDE TO START EXPORT BUSINESS

VEDANT BORLE

Author's Note

Firstly, EXPORTS BUSINESS: WHY? Because people find this to be a profitable endeavor? True? For the majority of readers, that may be the primary idea. But I had no information about it till I was close to graduating. I graduated and obtained my first job in a technology-based Freight forwarding company. I had no idea about freight forwarders at the time, but I was familiar with export and import terms and how people are doing good in the export-import business making a lot of money and contributing to the economy. And my desire to learn more about it made me enjoy my first job and assisted me in writing this book. From this I want to explain: How can you start your Export Business in India? In the coming chapters.

Now you must be thinking about What Freight Forwarder/ Forwarding which I mentioned above. What do they do? What is their work in Export and Import?- The freight forwarder works with businesses, importers, and exporters to ensure that items are transported in the safest, most efficient, and cost-effective manner possible. A freight forwarder handles the logistics and ensures that all bases are covered when transporting products from point A to point B anywhere in the world, as we will discuss in detail in the next chapters. Once you have entered into the business with all the knowledge, marketing, licenses, and products., freight forwarders make the exporter's and importer's job easier in areas such as documentation, consultation, tracking, operations, and many more that we will discuss in future chapters. Otherwise, I have observed a lot of people who are beginning their first export/import and are unsure of what to do next or how to handle the situation when starting their first export/import business. Many of them end up losing a lot of money due to paying large penalties and other expenses, and they become depressed, get demotivated, and close their business never to return. For a better understanding of policies, procedures, containers, terms, documentation, banking, risk management, marketing, and other topics, let's start with the fundamentals.

We know that Exports are done via 2 major modes Air and Ocean. Over 80% of International trade in goods is carried over waves i.e. By Sea, and the number is significantly higher in most emerging and economically developing countries such as India. There was some imbalance among Indian exporters during the COVID-19 pandemic. The Indian government's Vocal for Local campaign exhorts Indians to buy local goods to promote economic development. By encouraging exporters and traders to prioritize and promote domestically produced items globally, the initiative helps domestic industries grow. So how do exports help in economic development? As we can see the high exports in the country are advantageous since they improve foreign exchange reserves, create employment opportunities, stimulate manufacturing, and raise government revenue. So if you are planning to start doing exports you are also contributing to your country's economic development.

You may be wondering where to begin, how should I begin, I don't have experience, money/investment, or product, I am a homemaker, student, working at a supply chain or goods forwarding company, and so on. As we all know, procrastination knows no bounds. Ninety percent of small manufacturers think that the "export business" is a very competitive, high-stakes sector that needs substantial funding 'Substantial Means Huge Investment'. If you don't change your perspective and take some risks, you will miss the possibility and opportunity to get your products into international markets. While working at a freight forwarding company, I saw numerous people who had a product but didn't know how to export it. Some people understand how to export but do not have a definite product. Some have fixed products and experience, yet they have several operational issues. However, people adapted to it and this made them better due to the urge to learn more about it. Most Aspiring Entrepreneurs believe that "Export Business" requires a lot of experience, being a manufacturer, and having a large office infrastructure. "Get out of the myth today, or else your export business will be just a dream" I've seen small traders and exporters in cities such as Mumbai, Pune, Nashik, Nagpur, Delhi, and Bangalore doing well and making lakhs of rupees every month as a profit in one shop measuring less than 50'x50'. Almost all small home businesses feel that the "Export business" is just for major manufacturers, that the process is difficult, and that no one will buy their product. Change your mindset to Export Business for All, or you may miss out on a global market for your products. Begin global marketing for your goods and turn the world upside down to raise market awareness. Nobody is big or small in this. Your only competitor is you. You must initially focus on learning, marketing, and improving your product and service. Other than this profit, rivalry, money, fame, and infrastructure, you will get in the process when you become a champion, a champion who will be glad not only when you succeed, but also when you fail and are in a bad stage and know how to tackle it.

Who can read this Book?

Are you a small, new-to-export manufacturer aiming to export your products worldwide, achieve exponential growth, and develop a Network to sell and do marketing of the product? Aspiring entrepreneurs interested in starting an export company, learning more about the industry, present and market trends, and where to begin. Many women are performing well in this business, excelling in the supply chain, freight forwarding, importing, and exporting a wide range of products abroad. One of my classmates imports and sells biotechnology products such as eye-checking machines as Refractometers and Retinoscopes in India and she is doing very great in that. In my first job, my boss was a woman, and I learned a lot from her. If you are a homemaker who wants to export your small product, wants to locate the proper market demand, and creates the ideal business model, and is looking for where to start. This book can be your ultimate startup guide for your export business. You've heard people talk about how to do the sexy part of exporting—the research, socializing, travel, and all of the marketing and sales stuff that people associate with the glamor of international trade.

But what I'd want to talk about is the glamorous as well as less glamorous side of exporting, which can help you get a 360-degree view when making decisions before beginning your export business. So 3-2-1 Let's Go!!

• • •

CHAPTER I

International Trade and Policies

Export policies are the collection of laws, rules, and regulations that govern the export of goods and services from one country to another. These policies typically aim to protect local industries, promote security, ensure compliance with international trade laws, and maintain trade balance. Export policies typically involve several elements, such as licensing and permissions, export promotion schemes, trade agreements, GST, customs duties and tariffs, quality standards and certifications, sanctions, and regulations. For global trade to run smoothly and legally, exporters must keep up with changes to export laws and regulations. For additional help in managing the complexity of export compliance, consulting with government trade agencies, practitioners, freight forwarders and trade associations might be helpful. This chapter is going to give you additional information on this topic as well as how to monitor and track these policies in a way that encourages thought and helps you understand how primary research is started.

1) Why International Trade?

Businesses can offer their products and services in new markets thanks to international trade, which boosts earnings and promotes business growth at a global level. So why are many countries involved with each other for the other countries' development? Because each nation's supply and demand are different, one nation facilitates trade with others by acting as a source of supplies, meeting that nation's needs, and vice versa.

International trade can be divided into three categories: export, import, and entrepot trade. Export is the shipment of goods that are sold overseas, or, to put it another way, the sending of goods by exporters of one country to another to satisfy their demands or make sales. Exporting is the sale of goods and services in foreign countries that are sourced or manufactured in the home country.

The inverse of exporting is importing. Importing is the process of purchasing goods and services from other countries and bringing them back into one's own country. Entrepot trade is essentially a transaction in which imported commodities are re-exported /exported with or without any additional processing or packaging. Entrepotis mostly refers to duty-free ports with a high volume of re-export trade. But now we only focus on export trade.

So why this Export trade, why should we do export? When the country imports more than it exports, a greater amount is taken out of the nation than is brought in via revenue from exports. As I previously stated, exports contribute to the country's economic progress. As we become the other country's supplier, we fulfill their requirements. When demand rises, supply rises as well. When supply increases, so does the amount of money that enters the country. Exporting may be profitable for many types of businesses. Sales rise quicker on average, more jobs are created, and people earn more than in non-exporting firms. Consider China, which is the world's largest exporter, doing more than $3.72 trillion in exports each year and ranking first since 2009, accounting for almost 14% of global exports. So why not India? Just like China, India has also started focusing on human capital development and will soon be the superpower overtaking China in all aspects.

So how India is focusing on Human Capital Development and How it is helping Exporting Businesses?

Workers who are skilled and educated are more productive and efficient. This has contributed to increased output in the manufacturing and export sectors. Productivity growth has also contributed to the country's growth. So the Indian government has focused on human capital development on a large scale to increase development in all aspects like advancement in the training of technical and non-technical things, creativity, social well-being, equality, increased productivity in Manufacturing, and higher rates of involvement, all of which contribute to economic advancement. The government is assisting people by providing training, financial assistance, tax relief, encouraging and promoting foreign direct investment, and encouraging people to go from local to global and start exporting. People in India have great skills to develop a product and go global, as the government is helping them in all aspects. We will see in our coming chapters how it can be done on a huge scale.

2) India's Foreign Trade Policy

The DGFT established the Foreign Trade Policy, which is a set of rules and regulations about the import and export of products within India. Every five years, the Ministry of Commerce and Industry of the Government of India releases the Export-Import Policy. Developing export potential, enhancing export performance, promoting international commerce, and establishing a positive balance of payments are the objectives of this policy. Please be aware, though, that additions and alterations may have been made since then, and trade policies are subject to change. I advise referring to the DGFT website or official government sources for the most up-to-date and precise information to make self-updates on what's going on in the market and what decisions are taken by the government for export business. For purposes of learning, let's examine the Indian international trade policy, which was most recently revised in January 2022. Therefore, in January 2022, India was in a position where many other nations were interested in investing in the country, since commercialization was picking up momentum following the COVID-19 pandemic, and India had recovered from it quickly. To capitalize on this numerous opportunities in the global market, as well as our economic relationship with other global nations, the government established laws and guidelines to encourage and promote exports. Promoting Exports was one of the key aims to encourage and promote exports and exporters from India. Several plans and incentives were put in place to help exporters. Like giving loans- Large scale/Small Scale, Discounts in taxes, and many more. Second, there were numerous obstacles encountered while exporting, such as documentation, procedural issues, and so on. Providing Incentives played a significant role in the strategy, with several incentive programs such as the Merchandise Exports from India Scheme (MEIS) and Services Exports from India Scheme (SEIS) implemented to benefit exporters. Another goal of the policy was to simplify and streamline export procedures to make it easier for enterprises, exporters, and small traders to engage in international trade. They make all of the procedures online, such as gate-in container documentation, customs clearing documentation, and insurance, and they also ensure shipping lines follow the procedures and make use of technology. This technology resulted in the Trade Facilitation Measures policy- An important part was the use of trade facilitation measures, such as the use of technology to speed clearances and eliminate paperwork. Another priority was to facilitate imports. Although encouraging exports is the main goal, the strategy also considered importers' requirements to ensure a fair approach to international trade. Because a large number of people who do export also do import. I've observed a lot of other Indian manufacturing firms importing raw materials from other countries, creating products, and exporting them to other nations. Which, for the time being, is a different business narrative. Encouraging import and export results in more jobs being created. Boosting Employment: By encouraging exports, the effort aimed to increase employment prospects and job creation. A large number of Special Economic Zones (SEZs) were established to promote the manufacturing sector. SEZs were crucial in the FTP by providing an atmosphere that was favorable to business operations, along with certain exemptions and incentives. Using the pharmaceutical enterprises in Pithampur, Indore as an example, customs clearance was completed electronically in the SEZ plant; there was no need to repeat the process on the port or the ICD. Customs and/or preventative officers are always on hand to assist with SEZ clearance. Also, there is hassle-free documentation because everything is done online thanks to technology. Companies have offices in places like Chennai, Pune and Mumbai. However, why is Pithampur, Indore, a production hub for them? Because of the available resources, Tax incentives, a need to create jobs at a reasonable cost, etc. Trade agreements that the Indian government has made in connection to that nation include: To improve market access for Indian goods and services, the policy took into account negotiations, participation in international trade agreements, and joint ventures. Trade agreements that the Indian government has made in connection to that nation include: To improve market access for Indian goods and services, the policy took into account negotiations, participation in international trade agreements, and joint ventures. Trade agreements fall into many further areas. Regional trade agreements (RTAs), bilateral investment treaties (BITs), WTO agreements, suspension agreements, and intellectual property (IP) agreements are some of the primary trade agreements that are now in use among nations. India is a signatory to six International Free Trade Agreement limited coverage preferential trade agreements, including the SAARC Preferential Trade Agreement (SAPTA), the Asia Pacific Trade Agreement (APTA), and the Global System of Trade Preferences (GSTP). PTAs between India and Chile, MERCOSUR, and Afghanistan. Several free trade agreements exist with various nations. India is in the process of negotiating free trade agreements (FTAs) with the UK, Canada, EU, and Israel.

Every five years, a lot more international trade policies will be introduced. Thus, stay current on your own using this knowledge. Keep in mind that trade policies are dynamic and are subject to modification in response to government agendas, geopolitical events, and economic situations. Therefore, for the most recent information on India's Foreign Trade Policy, it's important to check out the most recent documents and statements from the pertinent authorities. It is therefore essential to refer to the most recent documents and announcements from the relevant agencies, such as DGFT and India's International Trade Dashboard, for the most up-to-date information on India's Foreign Trade Policy.

3) India's International Trade Dashboard

Continuing to our next topic to learn more about the International Trade Dashboard for India. Any exporter or importer can receive a daily update on policies, regulations, and news through this dashboard, which is quite helpful. Since they may change depending on a nation's economic standing, foreign policy, geopolitical factors, etc. Official sources including the Ministry of Commerce and Industry, Government of India, Directorate General of Foreign Trade (DGFT), and Customs Department for India can be accessed to obtain information about India's international trade. A section of the official website is devoted to trade data, such as imports and exports. Trade-related data and policies are frequently published on these sites. Finally, for aggregated trade data, you may turn to international organizations such as the International Trade Centre (ITC) or the World Trade Organisation (WTO). I suggest beginning with Trade Statistics at dashboard.commerce.gov.in. In terms of the components of an international trade dashboard, such a dashboard often comprises some features, as shown below.

Go to the website and Navigate the Trade dashboard. There are numerous tabs on the dashboard, including commodity-wise, territory-wise, and item-wise statistics and many more. Examine every tab. Simply select the country, financial year, and other filters. We will obtain comprehensive data with graphs regarding the total amount in USD, measured in tonnes, of business we do in exports to the nation. Visit this page often to stay informed. And from there, you'll be able to see several significant export ideas and themes in the market.

What will you see?

Trade Balance:- This shows how the values of imports and exports vary from nation to nation. A trade surplus is indicated by a positive balance, and a trade deficit is indicated by a negative balance. What is a trade surplus? It is the difference between the value of a country's exports and imports. What is a trade deficit, then? It is the difference between the value of a nation's exports and the cost of its imports.

Top Export and Import Partners:- Information of the main countries that India traded with. Partners in import and export are included in this with data and charts.

Commodity-Wise Breakdown:- A comprehensive examination of imports and exports split down by product category or commodity. This can give insight into the kinds of products that drive the majority of global trade.

Trends Over Time:- Visual and graphical representations of trade trends over time, like comparisons between months or years.

Trade Policies and Regulations: Information on any modifications to tariffs, laws, or trade policies that could affect trade internationally.

Currency Exchange Rates:- Since many currencies are used in international trade, knowledge of exchange rates can be essential to understanding the transaction's economic environment. Remember that even when you book a container for export, you will deal in dollars. If your buyer is in Europe, however, you will deal with him in euros.

After reading about this topic, don't forget to look for the most recent current data. Generally speaking, it's a good idea to start by visiting the websites of international and government organizations.

4) India's Top Industries & Products for Export

India's economy is wide-ranging and growing, with several industries making major contributions to the country's exports. According to my latest information update from January 2022, the following are some of the leading Indian export sectors and goods:

1. **Starting with IT and Software exports:-** India is a key global hub for IT, and a significant portion of its exports come from software services like software development, IT outsourcing, and business process outsourcing (BPO). There's too much competition here, man—a lot of formidable IT rivals.

2. **Pharmaceuticals and Medicines:-** India is a major exporter of medicines and generic medications. The nation's export portfolio includes the pharmaceutical industry as a key component. A large number of small business owners and providers of pharmaceuticals began exporting medical supplies and other services like equipment. The primary concern of the Pharma Company is

temperature-controlled goods, which can be transported by air in a temperature-controlled box or via reefer containers across the ocean. Additionally, there is Envirotainer, which is used to quickly export pharmaceuticals under temperature control, But these are most costly as compared to the Ocean or Normal Air Export. Chennai, Pune, and Indore are the Hubs for Medicine Exports in India. India is ranked 14th in terms of value and third in terms of volume produced globally. India's pharmaceutical success story is a result of our highly skilled workforce, innovative manufacturing, strong infrastructure, cost competitiveness, and highly trained human capital. To engage in this. You can work as a dealer or broker for a pharmaceutical company, exporting modest/small amounts of their medicines/equipment to other nations. And have seen many people doing this on a huge scale as they have been doing this for many years around 15-20 Years. To sell this overseas, among other places, you will need various permissions from the government, a pharmaceutical company, and contacts abroad.

3. Textiles and Garments:- India's largest manufacturing sector is the textile and garment industry, which accounts for over 4% of the nation's GDP and over 14% of its annual export revenues. Textiles, clothing, and yarn are all part of India's traditional and significant export economy. The most commonly exported goods are silk waste, carpets, and natural silk yarn, then ready-made clothing and fabrics. The government of India has launched several initiatives, including trade exhibitions and fairs, to better promote the country's silk sector internationally. The top importing nations for Indian textiles are the United States (26.08%), Bangladesh (10.29%), the United Arab Emirates (6.45%), China (8.9%), the United Kingdom (18.86), and Other, which covers 205 Partner countries and accounts for almost 47%. It is a significant amount and market share. India, one of the world's top producers of clothing and textiles, is currently the world's second-largest manufacturer of clothing and textiles, after China. There will be one day when we overtake China in this also. For this several initiatives are taken by the Indian government to encourage SMEs, particularly qualified exporters, to enter foreign markets. These include the Rebate on State and Central Taxes and Levies (RoSCTL) Scheme, the Remission of Duties or Taxes on Export Products (RoDTEP) Scheme, and the Export Promotion Capital Goods (EPCG) Scheme. One of the sector's challenges is the inflation in the United States, our main buyer. An increase in cotton prices as a result of India's climate-related shortages. Additionally, the textile industry is slipping behind rival countries like Vietnam and Bangladesh. India's exports are less competitive than those of Vietnam and Bangladesh for several factors, including the Rupee exchange rate, absence of free trade agreements with Europe, small business size, cheaper workers, restrictive labor markets, and inadequate infrastructure. But with the support of such robust government policies and expertise, Indian textile SMEs can broaden their horizons and find new markets. The Indian government offers SMEs engaged in the export of textiles and clothing several benefits as I mentioned above. The goal of these incentives is to boost exports and help exporters compete and engage in the global markets.

4. Chemicals and Petrochemicals:- India is a major exporter of plastics, specialty chemicals, medicines, and other chemicals and petrochemical goods. Over half of India's exports are specialty chemicals, mostly agrochemicals, dyes, and pigments. More than 175 countries are the main export destinations for India's chemicals and chemical products, including China, the United States, Brazil, the Netherlands, Saudi Arabia, Indonesia, the United Arab Emirates, Japan, Germany, and others. Additionally, the sector began exporting to markets in Russia, Turkey, and Northeast Asian nations, including Taiwan, Macao, Hong Kong, Japan, Korea RP, and Mongolia. India is a significant supplier of organic chemicals, color intermediates, and dyes to China. By 2025, the nation's chemicals and petrochemicals sector, currently valued at US\$ 178 billion, is projected to grow to US\$ 300 billion. In India, the industry employs about two million people. The nation contributes 2.5% of the world's chemical sales and is ranked 14th in the world for chemical exports (excluding pharmaceuticals). India's chemical manufacturing industry is mostly focused on Gujarat and Maharashtra. Tamil Nadu and West Bengal are the two other significant producing states. To export chemicals, you will require several documents, including safety data sheets, hazard certificates, non-hazard certificates, and certificates of precaution. Certain chemicals are classified as HAZ or NON-HAZ, however, the exporter must indicate whether the chemical is NON-HAZ and whether there are any safety precautions that the shipping line or forwarder must take during execution. Even if some chemical compounds are prohibited or deregulated for export from India you have to undertake that also. The Basic Chemicals, Cosmetics, and Dyes Export Promotion Council (CHEMEXCIL) organizes numerous international exhibitions to encourage the export of chemical products. The council plays several important roles, including serving as an intermediary between the government and business, taking part in international exhibits, advising the government on policy, and offering industrial training and information transfer. In addition, the government has launched numerous other initiatives to support the growth and export of the chemical sector, including the Chemical Promotion and Development Scheme (CPDS) and PCPIR Policy 2020–35. Facilitating expansion in the chemical and petrochemical industry is the main goal of the CPDS. To go cautiously or slowly at first. Specialty chemicals, polymers, oleo chemicals, and other sanitary, medicinal, and cosmetic products are currently in high demand in India. Certain components will probably function better than others. You can test the efficacy of these products by exporting them in small quantities—one box or two drums—by air to neighboring nations such as Vietnam, Sri Lanka, Indonesia, the United Arab Emirates, and so on. If so, try it in other countries like the US, Brazil, and the UK as their air freight rates are typically greater than those of the nearby ones. Once you are proficient, make a long jump by sending by sea on a large scale.

5. Automobiles and Auto Parts:- India's exports are significantly impacted by the automotive sector, which includes the export of automobiles and auto parts. Without a doubt, starting a business exporting authentic automobile replacement parts is a fantastic concept. Automobile equipment, in reality, is eighth among India's top ten greatest exports, with a total value of $4.4 billion in exports. If you can truly thrive in the export of automobile spare parts and accessories, it may be a once-in-a-lifetime chance. Automobile parts include fuel tanks, saddlebags and panniers, mudguards and fenders, seats, helmets, steering wheels, horns, headlamp assemblies, grilles, diagnostic tools, silencers, mufflers, and baffles. Indian vendors may also allow personalization requests from overseas buyers. The states that export auto parts are Punjab, Haryana, Uttar Pradesh, Delhi, and Rajasthan. The US, UK, Germany, Australia, and Italy are the nations that contribute to the sales of auto parts from Indian vendors. It is anticipated that government subsidies, expanding domestic and global demand, and inexpensive access to raw materials will all play significant roles in growth. The automotive industry has benefited from the rising demand for cars, which has forced automakers to boost production levels to keep up with demand. In conclusion, India's export of auto spare components has been expanding quickly in recent years. Because of its affordable costs and premium parts, the business has been able to make a name for itself on the global stage. The industry is projected to maintain its growth trajectory in the upcoming years with the backing of the government and the availability of qualified workers.

6. Engineering Goods:- India exports a variety of engineering products, such as parts, machinery, and equipment. India has seen an increase in the export of engineering products to the US, Saudi Arabia, and the United Arab Emirates (UAE), and other small Asian countries. The primary products exported under the heading of "industrial machinery" include IC (internal combustion) engines and parts, as well as industrial machinery used in the dairy, food processing, textile, and molding industries as well as boilers, parts, valves, and ATMs. Determine the markets that your engineering items are aimed at. Think about things like possible export destination demand, competition, and regulatory constraints. Recognize the rules and laws about the export of engineering items. Getting an Importer-Exporter Code (IEC) from the Directorate General of Foreign Trade (DGFT) is part of this process. Make sure your engineering products meet the target market's technical requirements and standards. This might involve obtaining licenses or maintaining certain guidelines for the product. Put quality control procedures in place to adhere to global standards. By doing this, you can gain the trust of overseas customers and increase the marketability of your items. Make ties with agents, distributors, and prospective purchasers in the target markets. Engage in networking events, exhibitions, and trade shows to establish connections inside the sector. Find the most economical and effective shipping & logistics solutions like freight forwarders. Recognize freight forwarding, documentation needs, and customs processes if your engineering product is very big and can't be put in a normal 20ft or 40ft container. Here you can need an open-top container, Flat Rack, or some part of the ship to put your goods to send by ship. Other than this finance can be a crucial part in this to Create a pricing plan that takes rivals, market demand, and production costs into account. Specify the terms of payment, including the payment alternatives and modes. Assemble the invoices, packing lists, certificates of origin, and any other documents that the destination countries and India's customs authorities may demand for exports. To protect yourself against the possibility of nonpayment by overseas purchasers, think about getting export credit insurance. Examine your possibilities for funding your export endeavors. Banks and other financial institutions may provide finance for exports. You can also examine the policies and incentives offered by the government to promote exports. Verify that your engineering goods comply with the laws of the country where they are being sent if they are subject to sanitary or phytosanitary requirements. Keep up with any changes to international trade laws, rules, and market dynamics. Being flexible and always learning is essential in the fast-paced world of international trade.

7. Gems and Jewelry:- India is a significant exporter of jewelry made of gold, silver, and diamonds. India is one of the major players in the global market for jewelry and diamonds. The country has a long history of manufacturing and exporting a large variety of jewelry items, diamonds, and gemstones. The US, the UAE, Hong Kong, Belgium, and China are among the main export markets for Indian jewelry, gems, and diamonds. The Gem and Jewellery Export Promotion Council (GJEPC) is an important trade organization in India that is responsible for overseeing and advancing the export of gems and jewelry. They arrange trade exhibitions, offer assistance, and spread awareness of this industry. The Indian government has put in place several laws and programmes, such as export subsidies and programmes, to assist the jewelry and gems industry. There are several trends and difficulties in this sector, such as The jewelry and gems market has seen a rise in e-commerce, which has allowed companies to access customers around the world. Industry methods have been impacted by growing customer awareness of and demand for jewelry made using ethical materials and in a sustainable manner. Exchange rates across currencies can affect how competitive Indian jewelry and diamonds are globally. It is essential to uphold strict quality standards and receive pertinent certifications, such as those needed to sell diamonds through the process known as the Kimberley Process (To curb the trade in "conflict diamonds" and make sure that purchases of diamonds were not funding acts of violence by rebel groups and their allies who wanted to topple lawful governments, the states that produce diamonds in Southern Africa convened in Kimberley, South Africa, in May 2000. This meeting marked the beginning of the Kimberley Process).

8. Agriculture Product:- India exports rice, tea, spices, and other food items in addition to other agricultural goods. Cereals, fruits, vegetables, spices, and other agricultural items are among the many goods that India exports in large quantities. Numerous crops can be grown in the whole country due to its varied agro climatic conditions. Including both non-basmati and basmati rice, India is one of the world's top exporters of rice. Several countries use wheat as a staple grain, and India exports both common and durum wheat. India is also well-known for its wide variety of spices, which include, among others, turmeric, coriander, cumin, black pepper, and cardamom. Good quality fruits exported from India include pomegranates, oranges, bananas, grapes, and mangoes. Vegetables such as potatoes, tomatoes, onions, and others are exported to other countries like the Middle East, Africa, and other Asian countries. India is a significant producer and exporter of tea worldwide, specializing in Nilgiri, Darjeeling, and Assam teas. To meet demand worldwide, pulses including chickpeas, lentils, and peas are exported. Groundnuts, sesame seeds, and soybeans are a few of the oilseeds that India exports. So choose your agri-product based on your specialty, expertise, and availability. Just keep in mind that the export of perishable goods is very complex and must be fast, Otherwise, it will get rotten and get wasted. One of the many challenges and considerations that need to be made if Indian agricultural products are to be viewed favorably in international markets is maintaining constant quality. To be made aware of any tariffs, limitations, or barriers to trade in the targeted markets. Staying informed about crop and weather projections is crucial since they might have an impact on agricultural exports. You must remain up to date on and keep an eye on global price trends for agricultural commodities to make informed pricing decisions. Exporting agricultural products is particularly essential since they should mostly be shipped in temperature-controlled or reefer containers, especially fruits like bananas, grapes, and mangoes; vegetables include onions.

Iron, Steel, and Other Metals:- India exports steel and iron materials to several nations. India is a major exporter of steel, iron, and other metals. The sector makes a major contribution to international trade, and these exports are vital to the nation's economy. Iron and steel products, including semi-finished and finished steel products, are exported extensively from India. India exports aluminum and aluminum products, such as foils, sheets, and extruded goods. Among the metals exported are copper and copper products, including wires, cables, and tubes. India is a supplier of zinc and zinc-related items, such as alloys and sheets. India can export several metals, including nickel and items made from nickel. Ferroalloys are important exports, including ferrochrome, ferrosilicon, and ferromanganese.

9. Marine Products:- Fish and other seafood, as well as marine products, are important exports for India. India is an important exporter of marine products, and the economy of the country is heavily dependent on the seafood industry. A wide variety of marine products, such as fish, shrimp, squid, cuttlefish, and other seafood items, are exported from India. India ranks among the world's top exporters of prawns and shrimp. Exports of whiteleg shrimp, black tiger prawns, and other kinds are frequent. Many kinds of fish are exported, both frozen and fresh. This contains well-known species including ribbonfish, pomfret, and Indian mackerel. India exports Significant marine goods in both fresh and frozen versions are squid and cuttlefish. India exports a variety of marine products, including crabs and lobsters, particularly spiny lobsters. Additionally shipped are processed seafood goods like filets, fishmeal, and value-added items. With a share of around 27% among fish types, ribbonfish is the most exported fish species from India, followed by croaker (14%), pomfret (13%), jack (10%), and sole (3%). Twenty percent of India's total fish exports are to China, which is the country's primary importer of ribbon fish. For Indian marine products to be competitive globally, they must maintain a constant temperature and quality while doing exports of marine products. Keep up with evolving consumer tastes and industry trends related to seafood.

10. Other Raw Materials:- The popularity of specific raw materials can be influenced by factors such as the state of the market, global demand, and India's unique resources. India is well-known for exporting minerals and ores such as iron ore, bauxite, manganese ore, chromite, and limestone. India exports significant quantities of petroleum products, including refined petroleum. The leather business exports raw materials such as skins and hides. India also exports timber and wood products, including raw materials used in the construction and furniture industries. Semiconductors, electronic parts, circuit boards, and other components are transported to the electronics industry as raw materials. India also exports a wide range of plastic raw materials, including polymers, resins, and plastic granules with natural rubber and elastic materials.

To obtain the most recent information about India's export industries, it is important to examine more recent and focused data. Furthermore, it is your responsibility or take it as your homework after this topic ends to obtain trade data and reports from reliable sources like The Indian government's Ministry of Commerce and Industry, as well as global institutions like the World Trade Organisation (WTO), can offer current details on the country's exports. And decide which industry best suits you and can work with your field of expertise.

• • •

CHAPTER II

End-to-End Cycle

An end-to-end cycle comprising multiple steps, from the preliminary planning to the ultimate delivery of goods or services to a foreign market, comprises the export process. Exporting from India includes an end-to-end cycle with multiple steps that require meticulous planning, regulatory compliance, and collaboration with relevant players. This chapter will cover the complete cycle of Indian exports and the associated facts and information.

1) Export cycle in 14 Steps (Ocean)

There are several procedures involved in exporting goods from India by sea to guarantee the effective and seamless delivery of commodities to the targeted foreign markets. The following summarizes India's ocean-based export cycle:

1. Market Research and Planning

Strategic planning and thorough market research are essential when launching an export business in India. To identify the products you wish to export, you must identify potential products through market research. Take into account variables including market demand, competition, and legal constraints. Analyze your target market and Think about factors like the size of the market, potential expansion, and cultural quirks. Recognize the legal environment surrounding the products you have selected. Verify adherence to licensing requirements, quality standards, and export-import regulations. Examine your rivals within the Indian market. Determine their advantages, disadvantages, and positioning in the market. Licenses and permissions for import and export are required. The Directorate General of Foreign Trade (DGFT) is in charge of overseeing particular rules in India. Recognize the taxes and charges that apply to your products at customs. Learn how to use the Harmonised System (HS) codes and familiarize yourself with them. Choose an experienced logistics partner to ship your items. Consider transportation costs, shipping timeframes, and reliability. Warehouse planning allows for efficient storing of your goods before shipment. Consider location, storage capacity, and security. Financial planning is crucial as well to launch an ocean export business. Determine your price plan by considering production expenses, transportation costs, and market demand. Also, keep in mind that foreign exchange rates can have an impact on your profits. Consider using forward contracts to mitigate currency risk. Create clear payment terms with your buyers. Be careful of overseas payment methods and choose secure payment options. Learn in terms, which we will see in the next chapter. Marketing and marketing strategy is equally essential. Establish an online presence by creating a good website and using social media to market your products. Networking: Attend trade shows, exhibits, and networking events to meet possible buyers and partners. Make Use Of Digital Marketing: Use digital marketing methods to reach a larger audience. Consider digital marketing and search engine optimization (SEO). Large businesses always carry a higher risk than reward. What would happen if you received neither your break even nor your reward? Planning for risk management will be helpful in this situation. To guard against potential hazards such as damage or loss during transit, think about getting insurance coverage for your shipments. To make sure your contracts are strong and safeguard your interests, get legal counsel. Establishing connections with buyers, networks, and others involved in export trade. Think of collaborating with local suppliers, representatives, or agents who are familiar with the Indian market. Additionally, give top-notch customer service to foster enduring relationships and improve the reputation of your company. Additionally, keep informed of any changes to rules, industry trends, and Indian economic advancements to make changes in your plan accordingly, And you can adapt to the changes in the market as soon as possible.

2. Product Adoption and Compliance

Understanding the local market, regulations, and cultural subtleties is essential when adapting your product for export to

India. Product adaptation requires market research, packaging and labeling, size and specifications, product certification, and localized marketing.

Regarding market research, Understand the Indian market, including customer preferences, purchasing behaviors, and cultural variations. Identify your target audience and personalize your offering to their needs. Here it will help you who are your target audience and what changes can be done or required to meet the needs of your target market, based overseas which include time, season, quantity and quality too. Quality includes product quality as well as packing and labeling. Packaging and labeling ensure that your product packaging meets Indian rules and is culturally sensitive. To reach a larger audience, labeling should be in English as well as, if possible, local languages. Size and specifications must be included on your packaging and labeling. Adjust product sizes and specifications to reflect local preferences and requirements. Ensure that your product adheres to Indian quality and safety regulations. If you are currently running a home-based business and do not know the product certification, HSN code, and so on. Obtain information about the same. Obtain the appropriate certifications, such as Bureau of Indian Standards (BIS) accreditation for specific products. Check to see whether your goods require any further certifications from relevant authorities before exporting from India. Also, make sure your product is not banned or requires any documentation. Because export regulation paperwork differs from the documents required to obtain the imported product.When it comes to marketing, localized marketing is effective for export businesses from India. Tailor your marketing plan to reflect Indian culture and beliefs. Consider collaborating with local influencers or celebrities to increase brand recognition overseas.

The following part is Regulatory Compliance, with Customs Duties and Tariffs being the most important when it comes to compliance. Understand the appropriate customs duties and tariffs for your product category. Determine whether there are any trade agreements or preferences that could benefit your company. Also, consider GST. Adhere to India's GST requirements, which may differ based on the nature of your product. If you have not already done so, register for GST to ensure correct invoicing and tax compliance. Because it may generate complications during customs clearance at a specific port. Some products may require an export license/IE Code. Visit the Directorate General of Foreign Trade (DGFT) for special needs. Quality standards are essential in exporting. It ensures that your product meets Indian and global quality standards. Obtain relevant certificates such as BIS, FSSAI, and so on. Because some goods with any packaging can work in India but not in the other countries to which you are exporting. Labeling Requirements must be followed as per Indian labeling rules, which include mandatory information, font sizes, and languages. Include safety instructions, expiration dates, and other important information. Many countries have very strict environmental compliance requirements. So be aware of environmental regulations and restrictions, particularly for things that influence the environment. Comply with waste disposal and recycling regulations. Because other countries, besides India, have large and heavy penalties if your product's packaging does not comply with their environmental standards. Also, don't forget to obtain your Intellectual Property Rights. Protect your intellectual property by understanding and adhering to Indian laws. Register trademarks and patents as necessary. Local representation for promoting your goods can be difficult. Consider having a local representative or partner who understands the regulatory landscape and can help with compliance. Documentation is a crucial factor to consider during the export process. Please verify that all needed documentation, including invoices, certificates of origin, licenses, and shipping documents, is precise and satisfied and complete. So, after the export is completed and the money is in your bank account, the work is completed? NOOO WAY. Post-sale support is very important for expanding your business and obtaining additional orders for export. Provide enough customer support and after-sales service to foster trust and ensure compliance with consumer protection legislation.

3. Obtain Necessary Documents, Licenses, and Certificates

When exporting goods from India, you must comply with a number of legal and regulatory constraints. The specific documentation, licenses, and certificates necessary may differ depending on the nature of the commodities, destination country, and applicable restrictions. In this section, we will go over the overall overview of the main paperwork and licenses you may require before you begin your first export.

The first essential document/license is the IEC (Import-Export Code), which is a 10-digit code required by the Directorate General of Foreign Trade (DGFT) for exporting products from India. It is necessary for all export and import transactions. The next document is GST registration, which is essential for businesses that export goods. It is critical for complying with tax regulations. It's additionally essential to register with export promotion councils. You should think about registering with the appropriate Export Promotion Councils, depending on the kind of commodities you are exporting. These councils have the authority to advise and assist with particular items. You need to be informed and have your customs clearance documents ready. Create the appropriate customs clearance paperwork, including the shipment bill, packing list, and commercial invoice. The customs department receives the cargo bill for processing. In the documentation chapter, we will go over shipping bills and other documentation in more depth. Next is a Certificate of Origin. To determine the origin of the items, certain countries would need a Certificate of Origin. Usually, the appropriate chamber of commerce issues this. You must have a phytosanitary certificate. A phytosanitary certificate could be necessary if you are exporting agricultural or plant-based goods in order to guarantee that the goods fulfill the plant health regulations of the nation of import. Certain products require certificates of quality control and inspection. To comply with the standards of the importing nation, quality control or inspection certificates provided by the appropriate Indian authorities may be necessary. Also It's necessary to have specialized licenses and certificates. Depending on the products, you could require a particular license or certifications. Hazardous materials, for instance, might need permission from the Directorate General of Foreign Trade (DGFT) and other relevant authorities. A letter of credit is required, if applicable. You can utilize a Letter of Credit from the buyer's bank to guarantee payment if you are working with foreign buyers.A letter of credit is required, if applicable. You can utilize a Letter of Credit from the buyer's bank to guarantee payment if you are working with foreign buyers. Registration with the Export Promotion Council (where appropriate), To take advantage of incentives and perks, you might have to register with a particular Export Promotion Council, depending on the kind of items you sell. An insurance certificate is also an important document which can be required. Consider obtaining maritime insurance to safeguard the goods while they are being transported. In the event of loss or damage, you need to present your insurance certificate in order to file a claim for reimbursement. As is common knowledge, anything may go wrong when exporting products by ocean. A storm could occur, your container could be lost, the ship could sink, or a pirate attack could result in the loss of your cargo. Export Permit or Licence (if applicable), An export license from the DGFT can be necessary for some commodities. Verify whether your product is included in any prohibited categories.

It is essential to seek advice from experts in the field, such as customs officers, freight forwarders, legal professionals, and others with years of experience in this field, to make sure you adhere to all applicable laws and acquire the necessary documentation for your particular export situation. For the most recent information on export requirements and processes, local customs offices and the DGFT website are excellent sources of information.

4. Set Export Prices and Terms

Establishing the good's price is one of the trickiest tasks for a novice exporter. Setting a price is simpler when you are selling it domestically, but it is rather different when you are selling it overseas. It necessitates much greater consideration of several variables. You might not always be able to obtain the best value for the product by using market prices from outside. To draw customers, you must simultaneously stand out from the other businesses.

Prices may differ for different exporters. If you're a merchant exporter, for example, you'll need to list the price you paid for the product as well as all other expenses you incurred to get it to clients, such as shipping, storage, transportation, duties, customs, and tariffs. The production cost, which may be constant or variable, will be the starting point for pricing if you are a manufacturer exporter. Your total cost will increase if you incorporate the fixed component in the price of your goods.

Market conditions, production costs, competition, and legal requirements are just a few of the many variables that must be carefully taken into account when setting the export terms and prices for goods exported from India. The first step here in Export Prices is to conduct thorough market analysis to determine the demand for your product in the target market. Analyze your competitors' pricing methods and position your product accordingly. Calculate the total production cost, which includes manufacturing, packing, shipping, and overhead. Add a suitable profit margin to ensure long-term viability and growth. Costing is a key consideration while doing business. and make your cash flow obvious, as many people have gone bankrupt because they did not look into their cash flow properly and end up losing too much money. One of the many reasons for losing money is the exchange rate between the Indian Rupee (INR) and the target market's currency while exports from India. Because all business is done in USD from Shipping freight payments (If you are dealing directly with shipping line) to receive payment from the buyer. Be mindful of potential currency fluctuations and build a buffer into your pricing strategy. Account for any customs charges, taxes, or tariffs that may apply in the target market. Clearly indicate if these costs are included in the given price or are the buyer's obligation/

responsibility. In customs, many people lose too much money due to a lack of information and miscommunication in the form of penalties. Also will be dealing with the buyer, Be prepared to negotiate with possible and potential buyers. Have a clear idea of your bottom line price and any concessions you are willing to make. Choose appropriate Incoterms (International Commercial Terms) to describe the buyer's and seller's responsibilities and obligations for goods delivery. This will be discussed in further detail in the following chapter, Terms & Conditions.

Coming towards Export Terms, We know all the business runs on trust and credit, But do choose payment conditions, such as advance payment, letter of credit, open account, or a combination. Consider the buyer's financial stability and trust in the business relationship. Specify the mode of shipment (sea, air, or land) and shipping terms (FOB, CIF, EXW, etc.) with your buyer. Clearly define delivery schedules, packing needs, and any other relevant details. Clearly communicate your product's quality standards as well as any certifications they/the buyer may have. Align and ensure with the regulations and standards of the importing country. Prepare the essential export documentation, such as commercial invoices, packing lists, certificates of origin, and any other documents requested by the importing country/Buyer to Import your product to their country. Determine whether the goods will be transported insured, and if so, define the insurance terms- (Insurance is important- It is not a cost, it is coverage when the day is unacceptable and when there is a threat to your goods). Determine whether the goods will be transported insured, and if so, define the insurance terms.

It is essential to consider the market conditions and decide on the optimal pricing strategy. Some things to check for include being careful with the terms and conditions and fully understanding the cost components. Also, keep in mind that you do not have to adhere to a specific price strategy and should always strive to be adaptable, as the market is a dynamic being. Exporters should not be dependent on government subsidies. Make good use of the government's subsidies and make good use of it if it helps you. You should not totally rely on them. The government has the authority to remove or amend these subsidies at any moment, but you can still benefit from them. But it is not wise to rely on them. So make your decisions wisely.

5. Documentation and Contracts

In order to ensure a seamless and legally compliant process, exporting products from India requires a number of documents and contracts. However, what fundamental export paperwork is needed for overseas shipping—that is, exporting from India? It's the things you must do, and do well, in order to provide goods and create profit. Keeping that in mind, below are 11 export-specific standard shipping documents that you need to understand to ensure success.

1. Performa Invoice
2. Commercial Invoice
3. Packing List
4. Certificate of Origin
5. Country Specific Certificate
6. Certificate of Free Sale
7. Inland Bill of Lading
8. Ocean Bill of Lading
9. Air Waybill
10. Dangerous Goods Forms
11. Bank Draft

This is the main 11 documentation while doing exports from India. The documentation and processes that follow are just the tip of the iceberg! There is so much more to learn, including exclusive details, practical advice, and firsthand experience in the world of exporting. Now that you have a basic understanding of the documents required for export in India, you can begin the process of obtaining and compiling detailed information on them. And we'll go over this in depth in the next chapter of Documentation. There, you can see if the information you've gathered and I've mentioned in the chapter is common, or if you've missed anything. This is how you'll learn and work out.

6. Booking Cargo and Containerization

Booking a shipping container may appear to be an arduous and intimidating task. Arranging and booking an ocean freight/container shipment is simple and can be completed in several ways. You must gather all the information related to your shipment and decide whether to utilize a shipping line, a freight forwarder, or a freight marketplace.

When an order has been confirmed from an overseas buyer, it's time to begin the delivery procedure. You must consider a number of cargo, shipment, and container-related factors before you actually begin scheduling your containers.

These kinds of specifics are necessary because they will dictate the kind and quantity of containers you will need to reserve. It is advisable to try to prevent having to change a reservation later on because changes need additional work and carrier approval. Before you start booking, asses the following details: Cargo: Type, Dimensions, weight, special handling, load type; Shipment: Consignee, Destination, Permits and Documentation, Cargo Ready Date; Container: Type, Size, and Quantity *In the following chapter, we will look at several types of containers.

You can now begin the booking procedure after verifying the shipment, container, and cargo data. If you are an established shipper with legal contracts with shipping lines or carriers, you can book directly with them. If you're planning a spot-rate shipment or need to book containers to complete individual orders, you can do so through freight forwarders, shipping lines, or a freight marketplace.Booking through freight forwarders allows you to access different carriers and their associated services. This is because goods forwarders deal closely with a wide range of shipping companies and have access to unique prices and freight rates. Don't fall into low discounted prices of freights, See services and reputation of that forwarder is also important for your Valuable cargo safety. Furthermore, goods forwarders can provide end-to-end services. This means they may provide an effortless experience from container pickup at the point of origin to final delivery at the destination (door-to-door service). This may include the customs clearance, pre- and on-carriage, paperwork, tracking, and other services. A more innovative technique, which has gained significant traction in recent years, is to book your containers through a freight marketplace. Freight marketplaces are websites that compile shipping rates and information to provide users with a number of possibilities. However, take in mind that customer assistance may be less easy and focused via online freight marketplace than ordering through a goods forwarder or shipping company. Many experienced exporters choose to use freight marketplaces since they require little customer help during their shipments, whereas novice exporters require complete support during their shipments to avoid blunders. Once you've determined the appropriate container types and quantities, you'll need to supply essential shipping information. Without this information, freight forwarders, shipping lines, and freight marketplaces are unable to process your booking. Details such as shipper details, consignee details, cargo ready date, pick-up details, cargo type, notify party, vessel name, number of containers, and booking instructions.You will now need to decide which sailing to take. It's worth noting that this is one of the most significant pieces of information needed, as it serves as a basis for all following occurrences. You must pick the sailing (which is indicated in the sailing schedule; vessel name and voyage number), as well as the estimated departure and arrival dates and times - ETD, ETA, and Sail.

A booking confirmation, also known as a pro forma booking, is shown to you once you have finished the booking procedure and filled out all the necessary information. A booking confirmation acts like a receipt and provides all of the important information. Immediately following this step, you can be given payment choices according to how you reserve your containers. As soon as the shipping company confirms the booking, make sure the cargo and container are prepared for pickup. Your containers will be delivered for shipping on the day that you specified when your cargo is ready before the cut-off, as you did when making the booking. Check that the packaging for your goods is suitable for the sea and that, if palletized, the pallets are shrink-wrapped. This is crucial to prevent potential damage claims and to safeguard the cargo from harm during transit. You will receive updates from your freight forwarder, shipping line, or freight marketplace providers whenever the containers are picked up, gated-in or not, departed via vessel, how many days to move for transit etc. Remember that you can use a variety of websites to track your cargo containers or container ships. You can also track via a shipping lined website using Bill of Lading Number or Booking Number. After containers are picked-up, Customs Clearance and Pre-Shipment Clearance is an important task which we will see in the next chapter. And learn how it is important, Complicated, Cause to Penalty if made some mistake and all.

7. Customs-Clearance and Pre-Shipment Clearance

For exporters, navigating the procedure for customs clearance can present several difficulties. Businesses may overcome these obstacles and guarantee seamless customs clearance, reducing interruptions and optimizing effectiveness in global trade, by staying careful, obtaining expert aid, and keeping updated of customs regulations. Starting with the filing of a shipping bill and the related procedures, customs clearance of goods begins. But, there are a few requirements and shipping conditions we need to be aware of before an exporter attempts to obtain customs clearance for your goods. The import-export code, authorized foreign exchange dealer code, current account for duty drawback credit, and export license are the main ones. It is the exporter's duty to evaluate the tariff levied on their exported goods. When completing the shipping bill, it is expected that the accurate classification, rate of duty, and value of the products will be declared, along with a suitable claim of the exemption notification. The commercial invoice and packing list, the consular invoice, the certificate of origin, the insurance certificate, and other documents are created at this point. If you are doing clearance via your freight forwarder or CHA they are very expert in this, They will help you in every step from where to get documents to solve the situation.

In Pre-Shipment Clearance exporter will do obtain IEC Code, Classify Good, Prepare Exports documents like Commercial Invoice, Packing Goods, Bill of Lading, Certificate of Origin, Letter of Credit (If Applicable), Shipping Bill, Export License (If Applicable). Filling Shipping bills also happen in Pre Shipment clearance and pre-shipment documents. Customs Declaration, Customs Examination, Duty Payment must be done on/before customs clearance and Customs Certificate are issued by the authorities to ensure this particular good is ok to proceed for export from India.

Quality Control and Inspection is also done during pre-shipment to ensure to meet the quality standards of the particular good which also includes packaging of the goods too. And the particular goods are as per the regulation of our country as well as, as per destination country. Certain products, like as food items, Pharma or agricultural goods, must additionally get phytosanitary or health certificates from the appropriate authorities to verify that they adhere to the health and safety regulations of the nation of import.

If we summarize the Pre-shipment Process line-by-line:-

1. Obtain IEC Code (Mandatory).
2. Preparation of Exports Documents (All which are mentioned above).
3. Customs Outward Entry (To Submit Shipping Bill and other required documents).
4. Pre-Shipment Inspection If applicable (Pre-shipment inspection may be necessary for some products. If an inspection by an authorized agency is required by regulations, make arrangements for it.).
5. Booking Cargo Space from Forwarder/Shipping Line/ Marketplace.
6. Export Packaging as per regulation of the destination country.

7. Transportation of Containers to Port.
8. Submit Export General Manifest (EGM).

Customs Clearance Process:-

1. Customs Declaration from relevant customs authorities, Necessary documents like packing list, commercial invoice and shipping bill.
2. Customs Examination by customs authorities to ensure compliance with the regulations and verify the accuracy of the provided details of the goods.
3. Payments of duties. Please note that some goods are eligible for duty drawbacks or exceptions.
4. Electronic Data Interchange to verify all documents online.
5. Get NOC (Non Objection Certificate) (Before Goods Get Shipped).
6. Track your shipment.
7. Clearance at port of destination and release of goods.

Some Challenges one can face during Customs Clearance from India:-

1. Documentation error and correction.
2. Delays in Clearance.
3. Dealing with Inspection of goods by customs authorities.
4. Adhering to the customs regulation.

Effective export transactions in India require navigating the customs clearance procedures. Businesses may secure the seamless movement of goods across international borders and expedite the customs clearing process by knowing the requirements, obtaining accurate documentation, and adhering to customs rules. Obtaining expert guidance and remaining informed about customs regulations and protocols can greatly enhance the effectiveness of customs clearance procedures.

8. Transport to Port

There are various ways to transport goods from a plant to a port in India; the method used will depend on the kind of commodities, the distance, the urgency, and other criteria. This also applies to stuffing that is done in your manufacturing facility or at the port. If stuffing is being done in your factory, the transporter must pick up the container from the port or the closest ICD/dry the port, do customs clearance, seal it, and send it to the port or ICD for further processing. If you are stuffing at the port, you will bring your items to the port, choose an appropriate container there, and proceed with the stuffing and clearance. Everything in this process seems a little complicated. Don't worry, though; Forwarder and CHA can assist you in completing this process smoothly. All you need to do is make sure that all documents are handed in on time and within the allotted time frame.

Transportation can be divided in 2 types for Ocean Shipments:- By Road-Truck/Lorries and Railway. So when to select By Road-Truck/Lorries and Railway as an alternative. Waterways are not possible in India, It's only possible if your cargo comes under Project Cargo/Bulk Cargo. If your shipment is small and urgent, you may want to think about air transportation. However, the air option is regarded as the most expensive. If you do the initial portion by air and then transport it to a port and stuff it to port and go by sea, the process and documents get complicated. So exporters avoid it.

So, if your production facility is near a port, consider Nhava Sheva Port. If the facility is in Mumbai or Pune, consider trucking or lorries to deliver your goods or containers. If stuffing at Port-Lorry Truck is an acceptable alternative as per quantity of your goods. And if you perform stuffing at a plant and need to pick up a container, a truck is an appropriate solution as per your container size requirement. Trucks and lorries are Road transport commonly used for short to medium distance. Trucks or lorries can transfer goods between the factory and the nearest port.

Rail freight is an alternative offered by Indian Railways, which has a vast network that connects key industrial hubs to several ports. Rail transit is an affordable choice for long-distance transportation. If your facility is in Delhi, the nearest sea port is Mundra Port. You cannot take your container from Mundra port to Delhi and then back to Mundra. Or take the goods to Mundra and do stuffing there. These are the extremely horrible alternatives. The greatest solution is to use rail facilities. That is an ICD. The nearest ICD to Delhi is ICD Tughlakabad. So you can send your goods to ICD TKD for stuffing and clearance, and that container will be shipped to Mundra port by rail. You can also pick up the container from ICD TKD, go to the factory, conduct the stuffing and clearing, and return the container to ICD TKD. If we talk about the cost here, Rail cost is very lower than the transportation from Delhi to Mundra. Some customers who deal in pharmaceuticals and perishable goods prefer to transport their goods by road because this commodity requires a temperature-controlled container with continuous power supply, and time by rail may be delayed due to rail congestion, so they do not take a chance and prefer to spend more money rather than risk.

Freight forwarders, third-party logistics (3PL) companies, or any other logistics service will assist you with this process. They focus on managing enterprises' transportation and logistics needs. They can provide comprehensive solutions such as warehousing, transportation, and documents. When arranging transportation from a manufacturing facility to a port in India, it is critical to consider aspects such as the type of commodities, distance, infrastructure, and budget. In addition, regulations and documentation requirements for customs clearance should be considered. Collaboration with skilled and experienced logistics partners can help to optimize the transportation process and ensure that items are moved effectively and efficiently.

9. Port Operations

India has 12 main ports, some of which are under private ownership and others under central government authority. These ports are governed by their respective port trusts and authorities. Some of the major ports include Mumbai- Nhava Sheva, Mundra,

Chennai, Kolkata, Visakhapatnam, and Kochi. These main ports handle a large portion of the country's marine traffic and are outfitted with sophisticated infrastructure and facilities. The port authority manages all port operations. The port authority's key areas for infrastructure development include dredging, berth enlargement, container handling equipment installation, and improved connectivity to hinterland regions.

However, other than these processes, the last steps in the customs clearance process occur when goods arrive at the dock/port which also comes under port operations. When the items arrive at the dock, the person in charge at port endorses the quantity on the reverse of the checklist. The exporter/CHA presents this endorsed checklist to the customs officer when the products arrive at the dock area, along with original copies of the invoice, packing list, and other applicable documentation. Following that, the customs officer updates the system with the arriving goods, validates them, and asks if any changes are required. They also mark an electronic copy of the shipping bill and give it, along with the previously filed original documents, to the dock appraiser. The dock appraiser assigned the examination to a customs officer. As previously stated, customs can bypass examination norms and the RMS to check any export cargo, up to 100%, depending on valid intelligence or information. This applies to perishable cargo as well. Sometimes customs officers will request a manual check of the container. This is termed a sampling test. A representative sample from the shipment may be drawn and tested or checked for visual inspection, description, valuation, and so on, as directed by the appropriate official. The Export Order (LEO)/Shipping Bill is the green signal given by customs to the exporter when they are satisfied with the shipment's verification and examination. The exporter's copy of the shipping bill bears the endorsement "Shipped on Board " from the customs preventive officer, who also ensures preventive monitoring for the loading and stuffing of the container cargo. This happens only when the stuffing and clearance is done at the port. But other processes are the same as for stuffing at Factory or Port. As of right now, the system has saved the location of the container on the port, allowing the port authority and shipping line to load it into the specific vessel. The container is positioned at the port yard in accordance with the vessel schedule.

10. Loading and Shipments

To ship a container from India, ocean freight services are required. Your items will be shipped by sea, either as a less-than-container load (LCL) or a full container load. These two freight alternatives differ in terms of how your items are sent, how long the shipment takes, and how much it costs. And here the weights matter.

Ocean freight shipping containers come in typical sizes of 20 feet and 40 feet. LCL shipping is suited for goods of up to 15 CBM. For every package weighing less than 100kg, air freight is recommended because the pricing may be comparable. However, if the weight of the shipment exceeds 15 CBM, FCL shipping may be a more cost-effective choice.

FCL shipping does not require you to worry about the size or volume of your shipment. Because you are paying for the entire 20-foot or 40-foot container, you can ship any size or quantity that will fit in the typical unit.

Depending on the kind of goods, the loading technique, and the equipment available, loading a container can take a long time. For instance, loading a container with loose goods requires less time than loading one with packed goods. Additionally, using a crane to load a container with packed items takes less time than using a forklift.

When exporting products by sea, the weight of the container and its contents are crucial considerations. The container must be able to be safely hoisted by the ship's crane, and the shipment's overall weight cannot exceed the maximum payload for the vessel it is being shipped on. Since heavier shipments take more fuel to move, the weight of the products being carried will also have an impact on the transportation cost. Before planning a shipment, the weight of the items must be precisely estimated because overflowing a container might incur heavy fines. So beware of the same while loading the container. The loaded containers or packaged cargo containers are transported to the port terminal for additional processing. At the port terminal, the cargo is further handled, including, if applicable, container stacking and preparation for loading onto the vessel incase on non-stackable cargo/container. Loading a 20-foot container with loose cargo typically takes two hours, while loading a 40-foot container takes four hours. Loading a 20-foot container with packed merchandise takes roughly four hours, while loading a 40-foot container takes about eight. It takes around six hours to load a 20-foot container with a packed shipment using a crane, and about twelve hours to fill a 40-foot container with packed cargo. Once the cargo is loaded onto a cargo vessel headed for export. Cranes and other equipment are used throughout this operation to ensure effective and safe loading. Once the cargo is loaded, the vessel leaves the port and begins its journey to the destination port.

11. Voyage and Transit

Ships transport these containers from one nation to another while adhering to the stringent ETA, or anticipated time of arrival, regulations and schedules of the container shipping business. The shipment is in transit during the ocean voyage. Shipping companies or goods forwarders may offer tracking services to help exporters check the status of their consignments. Ensure that you have received your payment, whether it was pre-paid or according to your contract. And your buyer is prepared for clearance, having submitted all of the necessary documentation. Your shipment's transit time will differ depending on the cargo's destination and the shipping method you selected. Your goods can take anything from five to 58 days to arrive in the Middle East or the United States from India. Keep in mind that transportation timeframes may vary based on whether your cargo route is straight or involves many stops-Transhipment.

Managing an overseas movement is not an easy undertaking. It requires an extensive understanding of the maritime industry, including rules and customs requirements. A single error in the moving chain can cause the move to be delayed, increasing the cost for the clients. And this is handled and taken care of by shipping companies and freight forwarders to take care-off. Throughout this process, exporters keep in close contact with shipping firms, cargo forwarders, and other logistics partners to guarantee a smooth transfer of goods from the port of origin to the port of destination. To obtain a precise movement, the exporter needs to track their container online via the shipping line's website. All containers must be transported safely, and this is the responsibility of the crew and the ship's master. They are experts in their field who follow the guidelines established by the International Maritime Organisation (IMO), Therefore, don't worry about the things; instead, seek insurance when exporting your goods. This is crucial when the weather is terrible and the ship is sailing against the ocean's waves and pirates are playing around in Ocean.

12. Customs Clearance at Destination

Before departing from Origin port, the shipping lines and/or agents are required to file an Export General Manifest (EGM) to customs that includes the shipment bills. EGMs can be submitted both manually and electronically. When the ship reaches its destination, the cargo is removed from it. At the destination port, customs clearance is performed on the shipment. The documentation is checked by local customs officials, who also make sure that import laws are being followed. The ship docks at the port of the destination nation after being given the all-clear by the port and customs authorities. Dockworkers use gantry cranes, which are sophisticated equipment, to unload ship cargo containers. On the jetty, they load these containers into trucks that are parked next to the ships. Customs officials may perform a physical examination of the cargo to verify its contents against the submitted documents. This inspection is intended to guarantee that the imported products match the description on the shipping documentation.

Customs officials determine the required duties, taxes, and fees using the customs value, tariff classification, and other relevant considerations. Customs authorities receive payment for the imposed duties, taxes, and fees from the importer or their customs broker. Payment is normally paid prior to the release of goods. Once all required payments have been paid and customs personnel are satisfied with the documentation and compliance, they will issue a customs release or clearance, permitting the products to access the country's domestic market. The cleared cargo is then released for onward transit to the importer's premises or a designated delivery point, where it is delivered to the importer's Agent/Forwarder and finally to the buyer. Which is handled by the exporter or importer in accordance with the terms agreed upon. Exporters who are responsible for providing end-to-end services as per the decided incoterm must choose goods forwarders with a worldwide network and have destination services available at the destination port.

Customs officials have the authority to perform post-clearance audits to guarantee continued compliance, and importers may be mandated to preserve records and documentation for a predetermined amount of time. Additional inspections by other regulatory bodies (such health, safety, or environmental organizations) could be necessary depending on the type of commodities. It's crucial to remember that customs clearance processes might differ greatly between countries, and local laws might require particular requirements and documentation. To ensure a seamless clearance process, importers usually work with customs brokers or clearing agents who are conversant with the customs procedures in the destination nation.

Exporters should seek advice from experienced logistics experts or customs brokers as well as local customs officials and buyer/ importer at the destination for the most accurate and current information.

13. Distribution and Market Entry

In order to successfully enter the target market after exporting a good, and you only wanted to sell that goods in the foreign country, a strong distribution and market entry plan are essential. In-depth market research is necessary to comprehend the distribution routes, competition, trends, rules, and preferences of the target market. After your export is finished, you still need to expand and attract more foreign buyers. To do this, you'll need market research and a strong network of international business associates. To determine the best distribution routes for your product in the intended market, you will also require a distribution channel. Direct sales, distributors, wholesalers, retailers, e-commerce platforms, or a mix of various channels could all fall under this category.

You can also think about establishing partnerships with regional distributors, agents, or traders who already have networks and market knowledge. They can support you in navigating local laws, immigration processes, and peculiarities of culture. To prevent any legal problems or distribution delays, make sure that all import/ export laws, tariffs, and customs requirements in the target market are followed by you or your partnership enterprise in foreign. It is necessary to create a branding and marketing plan that is adapted to the tastes and cultural norms of the target market. This could involve localizing product packaging, promotions, and marketing materials. Strategies for market entry give businesses a road map for breaking into foreign markets.Companies will select the most effective strategy based on their goals and target market since there are numerous ways for them to sell their products internationally. Determining which market entry strategy will benefit your company the most might be aided by understanding the distinctions between them. A market entry strategy should be chosen after taking into account the size of the market, the level of competition, the regulatory landscape, and the resources at hand. Direct exporting, establishing subsidiaries, licensing agreements, and joint ventures are some of the options.

A diverse strategy is necessary for a successful export and worldwide sales plan. This involves choosing the best entry approach after carefully examining customer preferences, current sales channels, and the changing environment around distribution and marketing techniques. If there is no demand, you should consider where you can meet the demand by supplying supplies. In certain countries, your product must be in high demand, but in other regions, there may not be as much demand. If you use the Middle East or Africa as an example, all food products such as vegetables, grains, and cereals come from India exclusively. Due to India's large supply and the Africa and Middle East region's extremely high demand. Each of these elements affects how buyers make purchases. It is not unusual for some brands to be more favored by consumers in particular regions of the nation or elsewhere. You may position yourself for success in the Indian market by tailoring your retail approach, such as by developing digital appeal, localizing marketing efforts, and innovating new products you can design for your target market in that particular country. You may improve your chances of exporting your products to new markets by properly organizing and carrying out your distribution and market entry strategy.

14. After-Sales Support

Build trust and loyalty with your consumers by offering exceptional after-sales care and support. This will encourage repeat business and positive word-of-mouth recommendations. The primary advantages of providing after-sales support or assistance to a foreign buyer include: Oversee service quality directly, manage distribution and warehousing effectively with a partner buyer or distributor, and expedite and shorten delivery times if a foreign customer requests additional products from you following a previous dispatch. Improved client interactions can provide an advantage over competitors in the Indian market. Since overseas buyers have numerous options from China or India for the same product. Therefore, in order to keep up a good relationship, offer them a formal visit in their home country or invite them to visit India, and give them significant price cuts/discounts will work here. Continuously evaluate trends in the market, customer feedback and opinion, and sales performance to determine any changes to your distribution and market entry plan.

This concludes the 14-step export cycle. I hope you understand. Following these procedures and efficiently managing each stage of the export process allows enterprises to successfully export goods from India to global markets while adhering to regulatory standards and giving value to clients.

• • •

CHAPTER III

Containers and Stuffing Options

1) Types of Containers

The most essential component of trade, transportation, and the shipping business are container. These containers hold a variety of goods that needs to be transported by all container/cargo ships across the globe. The dimensions, structure, materials, construction, and other characteristics of container units might change based on the kind of goods being shipped or the specific services required. Today, a variety of shipping containers are employed to fulfill the needs of various cargo shipping situations. In this chapter we will see the few common kinds of containers which are used for exports from India to export good all over the world.

1. Standard Dry Container

The most popular type of container used in the shipping industry is the dry storage container. The most popular kind of containers for transporting dry products are these. They are available in typical lengths of 20 feet and 40 feet, with differences in height and capacity. These containers are not appropriate for transporting food or chemicals that need to be refrigerated because they do not support temperature controls. Globally, there are over seventeen million intermodal containers in use, and shipping containers carry a significant portion of the long-haul freight produced by international trade. Their creation significantly decreased the cost of long-distance trade by transferring commodities, which was a crucial factor in the globalisation of commerce in the second half of the 20th century.

LABELS	DIMENSIONS
INSIDE LENGTH	5.895 m
INSIDE WIDTH	2.350 m
INSIDE HEIGHT	2.392 m
DOOR WIDTH	2.349 m
DOOR HEIGHT	2.292 m
CAPACITY	33 m^3
TARE WEIGHT	2230 Kgs
MAX CARGO WEIGHT	28230 Kgs ~ 28MT

1. 20 Ft Standard Container

One of the most widely used container sizes on the market is the 20-foot container. This container is ideal for little shipments that you have. The 20-foot is lightweight, making it simple to stack and load and unload quickly. For intermodal transport—which involves transferring cargo between trucks, railroads, and ships—this makes it an excellent choice.

LABELS	DIMENSIONS
INSIDE LENGTH	12.029 m
INSIDE WIDTH	2.350 m
INSIDE HEIGHT	2.392 m
DOOR WIDTH	2.340 m
DOOR HEIGHT	2.292 m
CAPACITY	67 m^3
TARE WEIGHT	3780 Kgs
MAX CARGO WEIGHT	26700 Kgs ~ 26.7 MT

2. 40Ft Standard Dry Container

Choose 40-ft container if your cargo will not fit inside a 20-ft container. These provide your cargo extra space. Because of this, a lot of businesses also utilize 40-foot containers for storage. Getting a single 40-ft container is also more economical than purchasing two 20-ft ones, as the price difference between the two is often just about 30% and you can send large quantity of commodity in one go.

LABELS	DIMENSIONS
INSIDE LENGTH	12.024 m
INSIDE WIDTH	2.350 m
INSIDE HEIGHT	2.697 m
DOOR WIDTH	2.340 m
DOOR HEIGHT	2.597 m
CAPACITY	76 m^3
TARE WEIGHT	4020 Kgs

3. 40Ft High Cube Container

In above image you can see the difference in the height of 40Ft standard container and 40Ft High Cube Container. The height differences between the 40-foot regular container and the 40-foot high cube container are shown in the above photograph. The most widely used high cube size on the market is the 40-foot high cube. This container is ideal if you have dry products that won't fit inside a standard 40-foot container. Additionally, the cost is typically just slightly higher or sometimes same than that of a typical 40-foot container.

2. Open Top Containers

The top of the container, or roof, is fully detachable, as the name implies. This feature facilitates the loading of over-height products that are often difficult to load from the front entrance. The product's advantages include towering machinery and tall, naturally occurring finished goods that can only be carried from rail bridges or cranes. Because the roofs of open-top containers are removable, loading freight from the top with cranes or other machinery is simple. They are often used for large or heavy loads that are too big to fit through regular container doors. This kind of container is essentially a top-less dry storage type. Bulk cargo loading is made possible by this. A plastic roof structure that is attached to the container using ropes and protects the interior from rain and other precipitation types exists. Since the cargo may extend over the top of the container, Overheight Frames handles this kind of equipment.

LABELS	DIMENSIONS
INSIDE LENGTH	5.888 m
INSIDE WIDTH	2.345 m
INSIDE HEIGHT	2.315 m
DOOR WIDTH	2.286 m
DOOR HEIGHT	2.184 m
CAPACITY	32 m^3
TARE WEIGHT	2250 Kgs
MAX CARGO WEIGHT	30480 Kgs ~ 30 MT

4. 20FT Open Top Container

There is an open top variant of the 20-foot container that is also available without a roof. A 20-foot open top container has a tarpaulin in place of the fixed top. With a width of 2.29 metres and a height of 2.25 metres, this kind of container is appropriate for big goods that is unable to enter and exit the typical door opening.

Alternatively, cargo can be loaded and unloaded from the open top of a 20-foot open-top container. Doors are typically located at both ends of open top containers to allow for flexible loading and unloading of the contents. The 20-foot open container is appropriate for heavy and bulky items like metal and wood.

LABELS	DIMENSIONS
INSIDE LENGTH	12.029 m
INSIDE WIDTH	2.342 m
INSIDE HEIGHT	2.326 m
DOOR WIDTH	2.341 m
DOOR HEIGHT	2.274 m
CAPACITY	65 m^3
TARE WEIGHT	2810 Kgs
MAX CARGO WEIGHT	26670 Kgs ~ 26.6 MT

5. 40FT Open Top Container

The 40-foot container is also available with an open-top option, which means it lacks a roof. This type of container, which has dimensions of 2.29 meters by 2.25 meters, is suitable for massive items that are too big to fit through a regular doorway.

Cargo in a 40ft open-top container can be loaded from above instead of through a door. Open-top containers usually have doors on both ends to make it easier to load and unload the contents of the container. Items that are large or industrial can be transported in an open 40-foot container. The cargo capacity of the container is 26,600 kg. The container is 11.81 meters long with a top opening of 2.22 meters.

3. Flat Rack Containers

Because the sides of flat rack containers fold up, loading and unloading cargo from the sides is made simple. They are perfect for moving vehicles, big equipment, or odd-shaped items. There are simply two sides and no top to a flat rack container. This creates space so that large objects can be placed on the rack from above or the side. The majority of flat rack containers have a length of 20 or 40 feet and are composed of steel for robustness and longevity. Certain flat rack containers have extra walls that may be fastened to the frame, and some are collapsible.

LABELS	DIMENSIONS
INSIDE LENGTH	5.698 m
INSIDE WIDTH	2.286 m
INSIDE HEIGHT	2.255 m
DOOR WIDTH	0 m
DOOR HEIGHT	0 m
CAPACITY	0 m^3
TARE WEIGHT	2500 Kgs
MAX CARGO WEIGHT	21500 Kgs ~ 21.5 MT

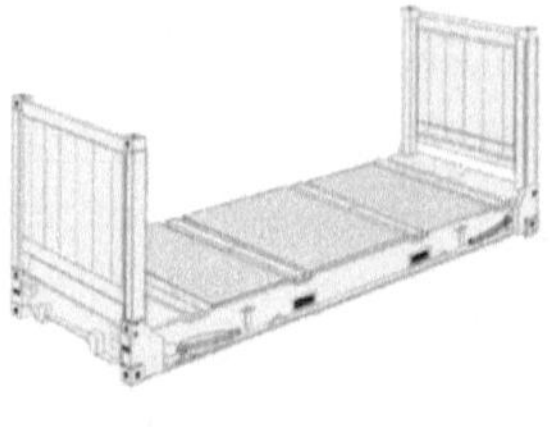

6. 20FT Flat Rack Container

Shipping large loads, particularly surplus or oversized items, is appropriate for a 20' flat rack container. Machines and pipelines, for example, can be transported. Some flat rack containers can also be folded up when not in use. The 20-foot flat rack container weighs 2,360 kg when pulled and has a volume of 32.7 cubic metres. The flat rack containers may handle greater weight because of their reduced tare weight in comparison to a container with more sides. The model of a flat rack container determines its cargo capacity. The inside dimensions of a 20-foot flat rack container are 2.35 metres on the inside and 5.70 metres on the inside. It is 2.24 metres in height.

LABELS	DIMENSIONS
INSIDE LENGTH	11.832 m
INSIDE WIDTH	2.228 m
INSIDE HEIGHT	1.981 m
DOOR WIDTH	0 m
DOOR HEIGHT	0 m
CAPACITY	0 m^3
TARE WEIGHT	4200 Kgs
MAX CARGO WEIGHT	40800 Kgs ~ 40 MT

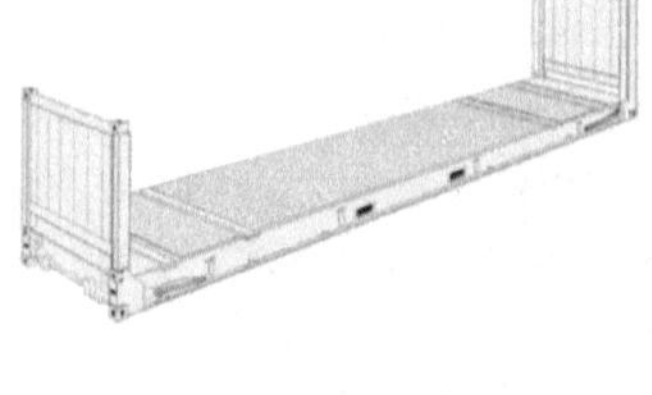

7. 40FT Flat Rack Container

Extra-large or bulky items can be moved in a 40' flat rack container. It can be used to move things like machinery and pipes. 40-foot flat rack containers weigh 4,900 kg tare and have a maximum load capacity of about 40,000 kg. The volume of a 40-foot flat rack is 51 m3. A flat rack can support greater weight than multi-sided containers because of its reduced tare weight. The inner length and width of the 40' flat rack container are 11.66 meters and 2.37 meters, respectively. It stands 2.28 meters tall. When not in use, some flat rack containers can be folded up.

3. Refrigerated Containers (Reefers)

These containers are suitable for transporting perishable items including fruits, vegetables, and pharmaceuticals since they have cooling systems that can maintain particular temperature ranges. When it comes to intermodal freight transport, a refrigerated container, also known as a reefer, is a container that is used for shipping items that is sensitive to temperature. Despite having a built-in refrigeration system, reefers still require external power, which might come from electrical power plugs also known as reefer points on the docks or port, container ships, or land-based sites like CFS or inside port. They can be powered by diesel generators or gensets that are attached to the container for use on road shipping from plant to the port and port to the last destination when being transported on a trailer or over rail wagon. Temperatures between -65 °C and 40 °C can be controlled in refrigerated containers.

LABELS	DIMENSIONS
INSIDE LENGTH	5.724 m
INSIDE WIDTH	2.286 m
INSIDE HEIGHT	2.014 m
DOOR WIDTH	2.286 m
DOOR HEIGHT	2.067 m
CAPACITY	26 m^3
TARE WEIGHT	2550 Kgs
MAX CARGO WEIGHT	21450 Kgs ~ 21.4 MT

8. 20FT Reefer Container

The purpose of the reefer container is for shipping chilled, frozen and refrigerated goods since it can maintain a consistent temperature for the contents. Medications, fruits, fish, meat, wine, dairy products, ice cream, and other frozen goods are commonly transported in reefer containers. For the products to remain fresh, a certain temperature is required. A reefer container has many cooling zones. One zone can maintain a temperature of 5°C, while other zones are designated for items that need to be kept at -18°C. It is possible to adjust the temperature between -30°C and +30°C. The cost of using a reefer container is higher since it needs fuel or power to operate. In general, 40FT Reefer containers are more in demand for the export of perishable commodities from India than this type of container, And 20-ft containers have an don't have excessive amount of inventory in India.

A 20-ft reefer container has a capacity of 27,490 kgs. The container is 2.25 metres tall and 2.29 metres wide inside. A 20-foot reefer container is 5.45 metres long and weighs around 2,900 kgs tare.

LABELS	DIMENSIONS
INSIDE LENGTH	11.840 m
INSIDE WIDTH	2.286 m
INSIDE HEIGHT	2.210 m
DOOR WIDTH	2.286 m
DOOR HEIGHT	2.195 m
CAPACITY	60 m^3
TARE WEIGHT	3850 Kgs
MAX CARGO WEIGHT	26630 Kgs ~ 26.6 MT

9. 40FT Reefer Container

The 40-ft refrigerated containers, also referred to as 40-foot high cube reefers, are taller than a typical 40-ft reefer. During transportation, a 40-foot standard/high cube reefer container can be programmed to maintain extremely low temperatures, which is useful for perishable food items and non-food goods like flowers and medications. To guarantee that the cargo is kept in ideal refrigerated conditions, the temperature is continuously monitored.

A reefer container, also known as a refrigerated container, is a container designed to maintain its chilled inside while being transported or stored. In addition to food products, reefer containers are also used for the transportation and storage of non-food items including Pharma products and flowers and plants.

There are 2,000 cubic feet, or 56.1 cubic meters, of storage space in a 40-ft reefer container. The T-floor within the container is designed to allow air circulation; with this kind of surface, the generator's air may be blown between the items in the container.

4. ISO Tank Container

Tank containers are made for shipping gases or liquids, including gasoline, chemicals, or food-grade commodities. They are equipped with cylindrical tanks that fit into a frame of a typical container. Transporting hazardous materials, gases, and liquids is done using cylindrical tank containers, sometimes referred to as tankers or ISO tanks. Before every tank gets permission to transport cargo, it is subjected to a detailed inspection. The ISO standards for strength, durability, and size must all be met by all tank containers. Liquid cargo such as foodstuffs (fruit juices, spirits, sweet oils) and chemicals (hazardous goods, like fuels, toxic compounds, and corrosion prevention agents) are transported in tank containers.

LABELS	DIMENSIONS
INSIDE LENGTH	6.058 m
INSIDE WIDTH	2.438 m
INSIDE HEIGHT	2.438 m
DOOR WIDTH	0 m
DOOR HEIGHT	0 m
CAPACITY	0 m^3
TARE WEIGHT	4190 Kgs
MAX CARGO WEIGHT	26290 Kgs ~ 26 MT

10. 20FT ISO Tank Container

LABELS	DIMENSIONS
INSIDE LENGTH	12.19 m
INSIDE WIDTH	2.44 m
INSIDE HEIGHT	2.59 m
DOOR WIDTH	0 m
DOOR HEIGHT	0 m
CAPACITY	0 m^3
TARE WEIGHT	3740 Kgs
MAX CARGO WEIGHT	30400 Kgs ~ 30 MT

11. 40FT ISO Tank Container

Since Flexitanks and ISO tank containers (20FT and 40FT ISO Tank) are frequently compared, This is added to make a comparison can be made based on the product type and the shipment's place of origin and destination. Bulk liquids are transported using both tank containers and flexitanks. There may be a better way or worse depending on what you are moving and the origin/destination.

Within the freight transportation sector, bulk liquid transportation is a significant sector, because it is very sensitive to transport and there is very inventory issue in India for ISO tanks. The most dependable and cost-effective mode of bulk liquid transportation may not be readily apparent, depending on the kind of product being shipped, its origin, and its final destination. Bulk liquids can be transported effectively using both flexitanks and ISO tank containers, but there are several key distinctions between the two. Flexitanks are economical dependent on the product's origin and destination and lack of hazard. These tanks must be moved back to their origin or to a location where tank container providers require them due to the significant cost of relocating tank containers back to the cargo's origin if there is no two-way business in the origin/destination. As a result, the price of ocean freight rises. Flexitanks might be very important in this situation to keep the freight advantage over tank containers.

These are only a few of the many kinds of containers available to export from India. Several factors, including the kind of material being transported, shipping specifications, and logistical concerns, influence the choice of container. Here are some considerations to make while choosing. Type of cargo by kind to find out if it's hazardous, huge, perishable, or general (dry). Use a normal shipping container for dry cargo. Additionally, use a reefer if your cargo is perishable or sensitive to temperature changes. The commodity's capacity, After you've decided what kind of equipment you'll need, you should consider the size of the container. You just need a 20-ft container if your shipment is small. In addition, the cost of shipping containers fluctuates frequently and is influenced by multiple factors, such as the location, the state of supply and demand, and the state of the market.

2) Container Stuffing Option

The process of packing merchandise into a shipping container is called container stuffing,while the process of removing cargo from a shipping container is known as de-stuffing. It is possible to use this process for both import and export. Stuffing and unstuffing containers has the primary benefit of minimising potential transportation-related damage from crushing, pressure, and movements.

There are two stuffing container possibilities. Not as much as the whole container load and container load. When the volume of your cargo is less than a full container, you can send it using the Less Than Container Load (LCL) method of stuffing. This implies that if your items are delicate or fragile, you may have to share space in the container with other products, which could be risky. If you have enough cargo to fill a container to the brim on your own, you are said to be filling a full container load (FCL). You are only charged for the entire container,And in LCL charges are depends on the volume-CBM, but in FCL as no other cargo will be storing their own belongings there is no chance of loss or damage from sharing storage. FCL is usually suggested over LCL if your items are especially delicate or need for special handling because it gives you more control over how each shipment is loaded and unloaded at the destination ports.

Sometimes, freight forwarders hold shipments under the LCL classification and combine multiple LCL shipments to form a "consolidation." In order to accomplish this, they reserve one FCL container and combine it with cargo that has been approved by other shippers. Following that, the commodities are arranged according to their transshipment or port of destination.

The shipper has to reserve at least one full container in order to transport an FCL shipment. Only a fraction of the container needs to be booked for an LCL shipment; a full container does not need to be reserved. Naturally, only one company will possess the products in an FCL transaction. Goods that are combined and owned by various companies may be present in LCL shipments.

Delivery of FCL occurs far faster than that of LCL. There is not a requirement to sort and unload the container at different delivery ports because the full container is reserved. Additionally, there is less chance of a delay at ports or at the hands of customs officials. More time is needed in the case of LCL for processing, document consolidation, and goods sorting. Additionally, the amount of time needed for loading and unloading may increase when dealing with LCL shipments. Also you cannot do factory stuffing in LCL shipment, while FCL can be done.

There can be less clarity on the handling and paperwork fees related to LCL cargoes than with FCL. Even if the freight rate is very little in comparison to FCL, it is still recommended to examine the terms in advance with the shipper as there can be additional terminal handling and paperwork fees. It is obvious that LCL is the only sensible choice for small cargo. The exporter must weigh the costs of both FCL and LCL, though, if the cargo volume is substantial. There will be haulage and destination service fees in addition to the goods. Even if the buyer pays these costs back, the price increase can still have an impact on future transactions. How beneficial LCL is for an exporter will also be determined by its cubic metre calculation. When it comes to FCL, the freight charge is based on the entire load of the container. However, the volume of the shipment is taken into account while calculating freight charges in LCL. When a weight exceeds a predetermined threshold, goods is calculated using weight rather than size.

Transit time is a major component. Only after the goods forwarder receives enough cargo to fill the container is the cargo crammed into it in an LCL shipment. The arrival of the cargo at the port of destination may be delayed if there are many trans-shipment ports for the cargo. Therefore, the exporter needs to know the date of container stuffing, the carrier route, the transshipment schedule, and the anticipated arrival date when choosing LCL. When the cargo volume is large or little, choosing between FCL and LCL is rather easy. However, an exporter must weigh the convenience and speed of the logistical procedure against the cost of the cargo when making a decision between the two.

3) Third Party Inspection

Third-party container inspection prior to shipment might be essential for Indian exporters to guarantee compliance to laws, standards of quality, and contractual obligations. Independent confirmation and evaluation of container conditions, cargo suitability, and adherence to relevant norms and regulations are offered by third-party inspection services. Quality inspection agencies, Certification bodies, Freight forwarder and logistics provider, Government agencies, Insurance companies, Independent inspection companies are the few third-party inspection done by the exporters in India before doing the export from India as consider as a pre-shipment inspection.

In India, there are numerous quality inspection companies that provide services to evaluate container condition and confirm adherence to quality requirements. These organisations might examine containers to make sure they are clean, structurally sound, and appropriate for the cargo they plan to load. They might also test for things like ventilation, temperature regulation, and moisture content.

As part of what freight forwarder consider all-inclusive of logistics solutions, a lot of freight forwarding businesses and logistics suppliers provide container inspection services. To guarantee appropriate sealing and documentation, these companies may verify containers at several points during the export process, such as pre-loading inspections, on-site inspections at ports or warehouses, and post-loading inspections.

For containers meant for export, certification services may be offered by organisations recognised by the appropriate authorities. These organisations have the authority to issue certifications attesting to the protection, safety condition, and adherence of containers to legal and international regulations. Certain cargo categories or destinations may require certification.

The regulatory control Indian Customs, government organisations in charge of trade, transportation, and customs enforcement occasionally check containers. Before approving the shipment of containers, these organizations may check that export laws, customs paperwork, and safety standards are being followed.

Independent inspection firms also play an important role in inspection that it focuses on testing and inspection of containers and could provide services specifically designed to meet the requirements of Indian exporters. These businesses may carry out thorough inspections that encompass things like pest management, structural soundness, cleanliness of the container, and adherence to international shipping laws.

As part of the risk assessment and underwriting procedure, insurance companies that offer marine cargo insurance may demand or provide container inspection services. The goal of inspections may be to find any potential dangers, weak points, or liabilities related to the state of the container and its contents.

To ensure the dependability and integrity of inspection results, exporters in India must choose trustworthy and approved third-party inspection companies. Maintaining the quality and safety of exported goods while reducing risks and adhering to rules can be achieved by exporters through collaboration with reliable inspection partners. Furthermore, exporters need to maintain close communication with their inspection providers in order to clarify inspection requirements, schedules, and any particular issues pertaining to exports of containers.

● ● ●

CHAPTER IV

Terms and Conditions

For a number of reasons, terms and conditions are essential in the export business. They create the framework for the transaction's legality, safeguarding both the importer and the exporter. Uncertainties or misunderstandings that may occur during or after the transaction can be resolved with the use of clear terms and conditions. They make certain that each party is aware of their obligations, rights, and responsibilities. This reduces the possibility of misunderstandings or incorrect interpretations of the agreement's provisions. The basis to execute export transactions effectively, fairly, and lawfully is provided by terms and conditions. They facilitate easy communication between exporters and importers, guarantee clarity and comprehension, and assist in risk management. Now let's see the terms and conditions on which you can negotiate.

1) Incoterm

The International Chamber of Commerce (ICC) maintains a set of rules known as Incoterms, or International Commercial Terms, which outline the obligations of the parties engaged in international trade. In addition, they have globally accepted guidelines that specify who is responsible for making payment arrangements and handling products during transportation, from the point of origin to the point of destination. Incoterms specify how shipments are to be delivered, who is responsible for any damage sustained during transit, who covers the cost of shipping, and what occurs in the event that a shipment goes awry. Incoterms are globally recognized definitions, but they are not interchangeable terms for global commerce procedures. As a trademark, it serves to distinguish the regulations created by the International Chamber of Commerce (ICC).

Understanding the appropriate Incoterms can be quite helpful for importers and exporters because it provides clarity and confidence.

By outlining each party's obligations, Incoterms reduce the chance of disagreements and delays. In addition, it helps cut expenses by lowering the chances of delays and avoiding unnecessary costs. Additionally, it lowers risks. Incoterms assist in defining who is responsible for what at each stage of a shipment, allowing both parties to handle risks more skillfully. Understanding the details of incoterm also helps to simplify interactions so that both parties can promote more understandable discussions at any stage of the shipping. By defining each party's responsibilities, Incoterms contribute to the uniformity and clarity of international commerce agreements. The primary Incoterms used in international trade are as follows and also refer to Incoterm chart while reading all incoterms:

	Any Transit Mode		Sea/Inland Waterway Transport				Any Transport Mode				
	EXW	FCA	FAS	FOB	CFR	CIF	CPT	CIP	DAP	DPU	DDP
	Ex Works	Free Carrier	Free Alongside Ship	Free On Board	Cost & Freight	Cost Insurance & Freight	Carriage Paid To	Carriage Insurance Paid To	Delivered at Place	Delivered at Place Unloaded	Delivered Duty Paid
Transfer of Risk	At Buyer's Disposal	On Buyer's Transport	Alongside Ship	On Board Vessel	On Board Vessel	On Board Vessel	At Carrier	At Carrier	At Named Place	At Named Place Unloaded	At Named Place
Charges/Fees											
Packaging	Seller	Seller	Seller	Seller	Seller	Seller	Seller	Seller	Seller	Seller	Seller
Loading Charges	Buyer	Seller	Seller	Seller	Seller	Seller	Seller	Seller	Seller	Seller	Seller
Delivery to Port/Place	Buyer	Seller	Seller	Seller	Seller	Seller	Seller	Seller	Seller	Seller	Seller
Export Duty, Taxes & Security Clearance	Buyer	Seller	Seller	Seller	Seller	Seller	Seller	Seller	Seller	Seller	Seller
Origin Terminal Charges	Buyer	Buyer	Seller	Seller	Seller	Seller	Seller	Seller	Seller	Seller	Seller
Loading on Carriage	Buyer	Buyer	Buyer	Seller	Seller	Seller	Seller	Seller	Seller	Seller	Seller
Carriage Charges	Buyer	Buyer	Buyer	Buyer	Seller	Seller	Seller	Seller	Seller	Seller	Seller
Insurance						Seller		Seller			
Destination Terminal Charges	Buyer	Buyer	Buyer	Buyer	Buyer	Buyer	Seller	Seller	Seller	Seller	Seller
Delivery to Destination	Buyer	Buyer	Buyer	Buyer	Buyer	Buyer	Buyer	Buyer	Buyer	Buyer	Seller
Import Duty, Taxes & Security Clearance	Buyer	Buyer	Buyer	Buyer	Buyer	Buyer	Buyer	Buyer	Buyer	Buyer	Seller

12. Incoterms Chart

1. EXW (Ex-Works)

The buyer/importer undertakes all responsibility for all transportation expenses, risk, and arrangements from the seller's location to the ultimate destination. The seller makes the products available at their premises. It is the seller's duty to arrange for the products to be picked up at the manufacturer or warehouse. The buyer is then solely responsible for all expenses and risks. This implies that most importers and exporters have to deal with a goods forwarder that handles everything from factory pickup to the end of the shipment. In EXW, Seller risk is the lowest, buyer risk is the highest, insurance is not provided, and freight costs are borne mostly by the buyer.

2. FCA (Free Carrier)

The seller ships the items to the buyer's designated carrier at the designated location after they have been approved for export. After the products are loaded onto the carrier, the buyer is in charge of all costs and risks. The seller is accountable for this part of the transaction. At a predetermined site, a seller and a buyer split the duties under FCA (Free Carrier). In terms of cost and risk allocation, it is halfway between the buyer-friendly DAP/DDP and the seller-friendly EXW. In FCA, buyer risk is highest, seller risk is lowest, insurance is not provided, and the buyer pays the majority of the freight costs.

3. CPT (Carriage Paid To)

At an agreed-upon destination, the seller delivers the products to the carrier or another person they designate. The risk of loss or damage after delivery to the carrier is not assumed by the seller, but they are still responsible for paying the shipping charges to the specified location. Upon delivery of the goods to the designated location, ownership passes to the buyer. In CPT, buyer risk is high, seller risk is low, insurance is not available, and freight costs are The seller is the one who pays the costs.

3. CIP (Carriage and Insurance Paid To)

Like CPT, however, the seller must additionally secure insurance to cover the buyer's risk of loss or damage while in transit. The seller arranges and covers the cost of insurance as well as transportation. In this case, the buyer has a higher risk than the seller, insurance is available (but only during the transit phase), and the freight cost is The seller is the one who pays the cost.

4. DPU (Delivered at Place Unloaded)

The goods must be delivered to the specified location and the shipping must be coordinated by the seller. It is also their responsibility to unload them. After the products are unloaded, the buyer assumes the risk. Here, the seller bears the greatest expense in terms of risk (highest), buyer risk (lowest), insurance (none), and freight.

5. DAP (Delivered at Place)

Until the goods are delivered to a specified location, the seller/ exporter is in charge of organizing the complete shipment. After delivery, the buyer assumes the risk. While import customs charges, fees, and taxes are the buyer's responsibility, the seller is in charge of clearing items for export. To sum up, DAP have Seller risk is high, buyer risk is low, insurance is not provided, and the seller is primarily accountable for freight costs.

6. DDP (Delivered Duty Paid)

The seller is in charge of the full shipping, which includes getting the items to the buyer's location and paying the fees associated with customs clearance. The seller has the greatest amount of liability under this incoterm. In this case, the seller is most financially responsible in terms of risk (highest), buyer risk (lowest), insurance (none), and seller-borne freight costs.

7. FAS (Free Alongside Ship)

The goods must be picked up by the seller from the factory, cleared for export, and delivered to a designated departure point, which is typically the ship loading dock. After the products are positioned next to the ship, the buyer has responsibility for the entire delivery process, including the primary leg of transit. Here From that point on, the buyer will be accountable for all expenses and risk of loss or damage. Here Buyer risk is high, seller risk is low. In terms of insurance and freight costs, the buyer is responsible.

8. FOB (Free on Board)

In FOB, At the port of shipment, the seller is in charge of the packaging, pickup, and delivery of the goods onto a vessel. Once the items are on board the vessel, the buyer has responsibility for the remaining portions of the journey. This is an Incoterm that assigns the buyer responsibility for all costs and hazards after the seller is responsible for delivering the goods onto the designated vessel. And Seller risk is moderate, and buyer risk is moderate. In terms of insurance and freight costs, the buyer is responsible.

9. CFR (Cost and Freight)

Shipping the products to the port of origin and putting them onto the vessel are the seller's responsibilities. In addition, they are in charge of getting to the final port, but they are not liable for that part of the transportation. Rather, the risk passes to the buyer at the time of goods' onboarding at the port of origin. Here in CFR, the risks for the seller and the buyer are medium; the insurance is NA; and the freight cost is the buyer pays the greatest sum.

10. CIF (Cost, Insurance, and Freight)

Similar to CFR, CFI includes the seller arranging and covering the cost of insurance for the goods while they are being transported to the port of destination. In CIF, the seller has the responsibility of transporting the products to the designated port and covering the expenses associated with goods and insurance. Here in CIF, the buyer carries the majority of the freight costs, the seller has a medium level of risk, and insurance is provided (but only during the main carriage phase).

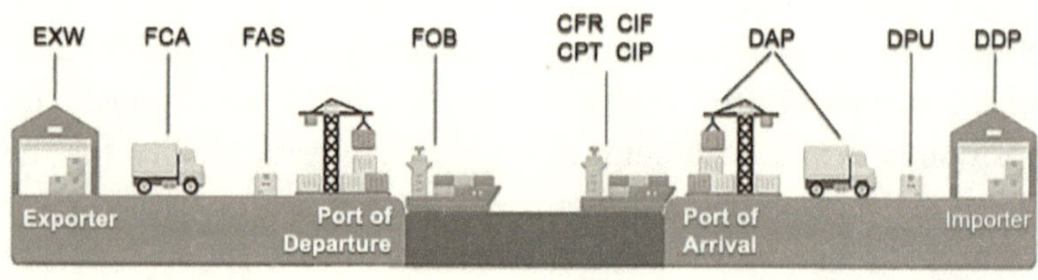

13. Use of Incoterm: For Transfer of Risk

To prevent misunderstandings and ensure that duties and expenses are properly stated for each party participating in the international trade transaction, it is essential that buyers and sellers both expressly state the selected Incoterms in their contracts. When choosing the right Incoterms for certain trade transactions, it's also a good idea to consult a lawyer or other expert or freight forwarder. This is because the choice can depend on several variables, including the type of commodities being traded, the route of transportation, and the parties' respective tolerance for risk.

2) Payment terms

An important task remains for the exporter after they have identified the appropriate buyers for their goods. The export terms of payment are as follows. Any trade must include this crucial step, wherein the exporting and importing parties agree on the final amount of payment. The conditions of the export payment can be decided upon by the buyer and seller through extensive negotiation. Invoices, which list the total cost of the goods as well as the selected mode of payment, carry some risk if you are a new exporter or an importer. Due to the additional factors of physical distance and differing rules and legalities between the two parties of countries, terms of payment in export also differ more and are riskier and sometimes costlier. For this reason, exporters and importers can benefit from a range of terms of payment in the export industry. They all differ from one another, but they all involve the mutual terms of the agreement. Some may be more advantageous to the importer, while others may be more advantageous to the exporter.

When entrepreneurs first begin exporting Indian goods globally, many Indian companies want or demand to be paid in full advance. If you do business this way, there is no risk of non-payment; yet, you run the risk of losing business to competitors who are prepared to provide customers with more favorable payment choices for the same product/commodity. The terms of the export payment are also based on the two parties prior trade history and relationship. This chapter outlines additional appealing payment options for you to consider when selecting a payment method for your export business.

1. Open Account

The open account payment term, which is more advantageous to the buyer or importer among the many terms of payment for exports, is based on trust. After the products are received, the payment is done. A credit period of a certain number of days is agreed upon in advance, and payment is due after that time. In international trade, an open account transaction is a transaction in which goods are transported and delivered ahead of the payment the due date, which is usually in 30, 60, or 90 days. Although open accounts carry some risk for exporters, clients may feel that this is the best option when it comes to costs and risks. The open account payment time presents challenges for an exporter even though it may benefit the buyer/importers by allowing them to pay after receiving the goods. The exporter has a large amount of time to handle their finances without the incoming revenue due to the payment delay. Small or cash-strapped firms may be especially affected by this liquidity crisis.

In certain cases, the open account strategy remains an effective choice despite its disadvantages. When there is little chance of default, parties with a history of mutual trust and strong connections frequently favor it. In addition, exporters might choose this approach if high-volume transactions are anticipated in the future, which would offset any short-term financial hardship with expected long-term benefits.

2. Documentary Collection

Documentary collection, this payment term in export transactions, entails the involvement of a third party, usually a bank. Both the importer and the exporter use their banks in this manner. Initially, the exporter ships the goods to the importer and sends the collection orders and shipping paperwork to their own bank. These documents, along with any relevant instructions, are then sent by the exporter's bank to the importer's bank. The importer pays its bank after the bank provides this information to it. In the end, a bank-to-bank transfer takes place before the exporter receives the money from the bank.

There are 2 types of documentary collections:-

Cash Against Documents: In this case, the buyer of the goods must pay "due at sight," which means they have to pay before their bank or the collecting bank releases the necessary documents. By doing this, payment to the exporter is guaranteed before the items are released to the importer.

Documents against acceptance: There is an arrangement for this payment term. This enables the buyer to pay after a specific time decided before. The exporter has agreed to a time draft, which they guarantee to follow. The bank releases the documentation to the buyer after acceptance.

Documentary collection still has some risks and difficulties even though it offers an organized and generally safe payment option for importers and exporters. While exporters must have trust that importers would keep their promises to pay on time, importers may find it difficult to guarantee timely payment to prevent delays in obtaining the goods. Therefore, making the most of documentary collections in export transactions requires close attention to the particular terms and conditions as well as the reliability of all parties involved.

3. Letter of Credit

The letter of credit is one of the most frequently used terms of payment for exports. This is because it is dependable and widely used in global trade. Under this arrangement, the buyer's bank issues a Letter of Credit, which serves as an assurance to the exporter. This letter of credit serves as an assurance that the seller will receive payment on time. When it is challenging to gather trustworthy credit information about a foreign buyer but the exporter is confident in the foreign bank of the buyer's creditworthiness, a Letter of Credit can be helpful. Because there is no payment obligation until the products have been dispatched as promised, a Letter of Credit also protects the buyer. In short, the letter of credit is a reliable and effective payment instrument in international trade, offering guarantees to both parties and allowing for quick and easy operations across borders.

4. Consignment

When an export involves a third-party distributor, the consignment kind of payment is applicable. This involves the exporter sending their goods to a foreign distributor, who sells them back them to the importer/buyer. The supplier only gets paid when the goods are sold to the final consumer when using the consignment method. It's comparable to using an open account to make payments. The entire procedure is similar to the open account payment method, in which trust is required. To reduce risks it's critical to select a reliable and recognized distributor. It's also a good idea to have insurance in place to protect against any potential losses.

5. Cash in Advance

The cash-in-advance payment option, which works as the opposite of an open account, allows the products to be sent only once the buyer has finished payment. For the same, a payment receipt needs to be presented. Although the importer or buyer bears a large risk, the exporter benefits greatly from this kind of payment. The cash-in-advance method has advantages and benefits for the exporter, but because of its inflexibility and cost implications, it could turn away potential customers. Thus, it may reduce exporter's access to markets and ability to compete while yet offering a safe payment method.

International trade transactions depend on the exporter choosing the appropriate terms of payment. Every approach has benefits and things to keep in mind, meeting the requirements and tastes of importers and exporters alike. Careful assessment and negotiation are crucial, regardless of the type of agreement a distributor-dependent consignment, a secure letter of credit, or an open account based on trust. Exporters may ensure seamless and mutually advantageous trade agreements by being well-informed and taking into account aspects like trust, risk tolerance, and financial stability while evaluating the intricacies of each payment term. Prioritizing transparency, communication, and compliance with conditions set forth is essential for building solid partnerships and enabling smooth cross-border transactions. Exporters can successfully negotiate the difficulties of payment terms and seize chances for expansion and success in the international market by using the appropriate strategy and diligence.

3) Negotiation

A combination of preparation, communication abilities, market awareness, and comprehension of the terms and conditions of the agreement are needed when negotiating in the area of exports. When it comes to negotiations, each party begins with an alternate viewpoint on what he or she intends to achieve. The term "conclusion" in negotiation refers to the ultimate agreement reached between the two parties, exporter and importer, on what they will achieve to conclude the deal and proceed with the shipment.

You must be well aware of the value you provide to the buyer and the reasons they should pick you over other sellers before you get into any negotiations. Your product or service's value proposition is the special set of features, benefits, and advantages that it offers to the client. It should include their objectives, challenges, and needs while demonstrating how you can support them in achieving them. You must investigate your buyer's market, industry, preferences, and pain areas in order to create a compelling value proposition. You must also customize your message to fit their particular circumstances. Understanding your value proposition can help you to emphasize your advantages over the competition and defend your pricing.

Before negotiating, You as an exporter should evaluate the company's existing situation in the market, including its strong and weak features, as part of the process of preparing for deal negotiations. SWOT analysis is used to do this (strength, weakness, opportunities, threats). You as an exporter can maximize your firm's strengths, minimize its weaknesses, be open to new possibilities and chances, and be prepared to negotiate in the face of threats by applying the SWOT approaches. The company may also attempt to find an equilibrium by emphasizing its strengths and offsetting its weaknesses.

The goal of negotiations is to reach a mutually advantageous agreement by allowing the two sides to trade demands, offers, compromises, agreements, and responsibilities when the time comes. You as an exporter, your company and your buyer will be ready to complete the deal if both follow the guidelines discussed during the negotiation.

Due diligence is also important during negotiation. It includes evaluating the potential foreign buyer's requirements, position, and financial stability. Information from the examination is used to determine whether or not to move on with negotiations and, if so, what subject matter and conditions to discuss and cover during negotiation. A portion of the necessary information regarding potential buyers might have appeared during the organization's analysis of the feasibility and risk of a particular trade effort. In order to lower risk, additional research into the financial standing and creditworthiness of a potential buyer may be necessary.

Pricing and terms of payment will be the main points of negotiation. In business conversations, pricing is typically the most delicate topic, so it should be delayed until after all other details have been worked out and decided upon. Some exporters purposefully overestimate their price quotations to overcome price objections. They can now begin negotiations with price cuts without having to assume any financial risk. The risk associated with this strategy is that it quickly shifts the focus of the negotiation to pricing concerns, neglecting other crucial elements of the marketing mix. Such initial reductions in pricing are typically followed by increased requests from buyers, which lowers the export transaction's profitability even further. The exporter should keep the buyer happy by offering them a lot of discounts, excellent service, credits, long-term assurance, guarantees, etc.

An exporter should make an early effort to determine the buyer's true interest in the product in order to prevent being faced with such expensive requests. This can be found by asking the right questions, but it also needs to be supported by prior research and other preparations made for the agreement and negotiation.

Following price negotiations, Payment terms should be negotiated to satisfy both the buyer's preferences and your cash flow considerations. Letters of credit (LC), open account, advance payment, and payment upon delivery are available options. Use safe payment options and, if required, credit insurance to reduce risks. And guarantee the customer that your product is reliable and of high quality. Assist with quality testing, supply samples, and, if necessary, provide warranties. Address any issues with the labeling, packing, or specifications of the product.

Agree on the terms of delivery, the shipment method (Ocean/Air), and the incoterms (such as FOB, CIF, and EXW). Make sure that the responsibilities, insurance coverage, and documentation needs are all understood. To prevent last-minute hustle, prepare for any problems or delays and forecast them.

Ensure to complete the paperwork for every term that was agreed upon. Write down all of the agreed-upon terms and conditions in a clear, complete sales contract. For help in adhering to export rules, international trade legislation, and dispute settlement procedures, consult a lawyer or any professional. And even after the deal is closed, stay in constant contact with the buyer. Seek information, deal with issues right away, and cultivate enduring connections to take advantage of future business chances.

Thus, how do you get a business? An agent can assist you in obtaining a business, but in exchange for his assistance, you must pay him a commission on each finished sale, deal, or shipment. Meeting with possible agents in the target market will present opportunities for the exporter to pursue commercial objectives that may not align with those of the other party.

Another traditional approach is to do business directly with importers/buyers based in another country. Similar to doing business through agents, the exporter of goods and the buyer/importer are the two unknown parties in the beginning phases of the business negotiation, even in cases of direct commercial negotiations. The importer often prefers to work exclusively with a specific brand of commodities, depending on the kind of product; in contrast, the exporter wants to reach as many importers, distributors, and dealers as possible to maximize its visibility.

Following these negotiation methods and meeting your buyers' individual needs will help you improve your bargaining skills and maximize the profitability of your export business.

• • •

CHAPTER V

Documentations

1) Commercial Documents

The use of commercial documents is essential to the smooth operation of global trade. It comprises numerous documents such as a bill of lading, bill of exchange, certificate of origin, packing list, proforma invoice, and commercial invoice. We are going to look at each one of them in detail and refer to the corresponding images as you read about the specific document.

1. Proforma Invoice

Everything in an export transaction often begins with an inquiry regarding one or more of your products. A quote request can be part of such an inquiry. If the request for a quote comes from a domestic customer, you most likely have a standard form to use. On the other hand, your quote would be given as a proforma invoice in an overseas transaction. You may apply for the necessary licenses, establish a letter of credit, arrange funding, and more with the help of a proforma invoice. A proforma invoice and a commercial invoice share many similarities. Proforma invoices specify The buyer and seller involved in the transaction, A thorough description of the goods, and the Date of expiration of the Proforma Invoice. The Harmonised System classification of those products, The price, The sale's payment term, which is commonly represented as one of the 11 current Incoterms, Delivery information, including how and where the goods will be delivered and how much it will cost, The currency used in the quote, whether it is US dollars or another currency.

PROFORMA INVOICE

PROFORMA INVOICE NO. & DATE	BUYER/CUSTOMER ADDRESS			
PURCHASE ORDER NO. & DATE				
QUOTATION REF.	DESTINATION PORT			
	DESTINATION COUNTRY			
PAYMENT TERMS	CURRENCY OF SALE			
MATERIAL				

SR.NO.	SIZE	NOS/UNIT	SET	RATE/SET (US DOLLAR)
				$ -
				$ -
				$ -
		TOTAL VALUE:		$ -
PACKING & FORWADING				$ -
		GRAND TOTAL:		$ -
		ADVANCE PAID		$ -
		PAYABLE		$ -
IN WORDS				

* Note:

XYZ PVT.LTD.

Designation :EXPORT MANAGER

Signature   :________________

14. Format of Proforma Invoice

2. Commercial Invoice

Once you've sent a proforma invoice to your international
prospect and received their order, you must prepare your goods
for shipment, which includes all essential documentation. The
commercial invoice contains the majority of information about the
complete export transaction, from beginning to end. Keep in mind

that the invoices you generate from your company's accounting or ERP system are accounting invoices used to collect payment, not export invoices. The commercial invoice could look like the proforma invoice you originally sent to your customer as a quote, but it should include extra information you were not aware of. For example, after you have the commercial invoice, you will most likely have an order number, purchase order number, or another type of customer reference number, as well as extra banking and payment information. Include any essential maritime insurance information, as well as any other details that will ensure the products are delivered on time and your customer pays in full.

COMMERCIAL INVOICE

SELLER		INVOICE NUMBER		DATE
		CUSTOMER REFERENCE NUMBER		DATE
SOLD TO		TERMS OF SALE/		
		TERMS OF PAYMENT		
SHIP TO		CURRENCY OF SETTLEMENT		
		MODE OF SHIPMENT		BILL OF LADING/AWB

QTY	PRODUCT DESCRIPTION AND HARMONIZED CODE	UNIT OF MEASURE	UNIT PRICE	TOTAL PRICE

PACKAGE MARKS	TOTAL COMMERCIAL VALUE	
	MISC CHARGES (PACKING, INSURANCCE, ETC)	
	TOTAL INVOICE VALUE	
CERTIFICATIONS	I CERTIFY THA THTE STATED EXPORT PROCES AND DESCRIPTION OF GOODS ARE TRUE AND CORRECT	
	SIGNED	
	TITLE_______________	

15. Format of Commercial Invoice

3. Packing List

An export packing list may be more thorough than the packing list or packing slip you use for domestic shipments. It can be used in the following ways. Your freight forwarder may utilize the information on the packing list to construct the shipment's bills of lading. A bank may request a thorough packing list as part of the paperwork you produce to be paid under a letter of credit. The destination country may utilize the packing list to locate specific packed items for inspection. It's far preferable that they know which box to open or pallet to unwrap rather than having to search the entire shipment. The packing list lists the contents in the shipment, including the net and gross weight and dimensions of the packages, as well as any additional instructions for assuring the goods' safe transit to their final destination. If cargo is lost or damaged, a packing list is necessary to file an insurance claim, and it is also utilized if the carrier and the exporter disagree on the cargo's weight or dimensions.

PACKING LIST

Exporter	Invoice No. & Date	Exporter's Ref.
	Buyer's Order No. & Date	
	Other Reference (s)	IEC NO:
Consignee	Buyer (if other than consignee)	

	Country of Origin of Goods INDIA	Country of Final Destination
	Terms of Delivery and Payment	

Pre-Carriage by	Place of Receipt by Pre-carrier	
Vessel/Flight No.	Port of Loading	CIF
Port of Discharge	Final Distination	

Marks & Nos./	No. & Kind of Pkgs	Description of Goods	Quanity	Size	Total Pcs

	Signature & Date
Declaration: We declare that this invoice shows the actual price of the goods described and that all particulars are true and correct.	Authorised Signature

16. Format of Packing List

4. Certificate of Origin

To find out where the items originated, multiple countries want a certificate of origin. Typically, a semi-official entity such as a chamber of commerce or a country's consulate office must sign these certificates of origin. Even if your commercial invoice specifies the country of origin, you might still need to provide a certificate of origin. A chamber of commerce usually charges you a fee to sign and stamp your certificate or demands that you become a member in order to do so. A completed form must be delivered to the chamber office so that they can sign and stamp it on your behalf.

Electronic certificates of origin (eCOs) are becoming the preferred method for shipping for businesses instead of the labor-intensive practice of hand-delivering a certificate of origin to a chamber of commerce for certification or depending on pricey courier services. An electronic certificate of origin (eCO) can be issued more quickly, gives you the opportunity to send the certificate to the importer electronically, and can be registered with the International Chamber of Commerce to give it greater credibility.

Certificate of Origin

Exporter Name and Address		Blanket Period: (DD/MM/YYYY) FROM:				
Tax Identification Number		TO:				
Producer Name and Address		Importer Name and Address:				
Tax Identification Number:		Tax Identification Number:				
Description of Good(s)		TARRIF CLASSIFICATION NUMBER	PREFERENCE CREITERION	PRODUCER	NET COST	COUNTRY OF ORIGIN

I CERTIFY THAT:

- Information provided in this certificate is based on facts and is accurate and I assume the responsibility for proving such representations. I understand that I am liable for any false statement or material omission made on or in concern with this document.
- I agree to maintain and present upon request documentation necessary to support this certificate and to inform, in writing, al persons to whom this certificate was given of any changes that would affect accuracy or validity of this certificate.
- This certificate consists of ___________________ pages including all attachments

Authorized Signature:		COMPANY:	
Name: (Print or Type)		TITLE:	
Date: DD/MM/YYYY	Ph: xxxxxxxxxxxxxxx	Fax: xxxxxxxxxxxxxxxxxx	Customs Form:

17. Format of Certificate of Origin

5. Bill of Lading

A bill of lading is a legally binding document that gives the shipper and the carrier all the information they need to properly process the shipment. For this reason, it is very important. This suggests that all parties concerned will go to considerable lengths to verify the document's accuracy and that it can be used as evidence in court if necessary. A bill of lading serves as conclusive evidence of shipment. A bill of lading additionally facilitates the separation of tasks, which is an essential component of an organization's internal control framework designed to prevent theft.

Ocean Bill of Lading

Exporter (Name and address including ZIP code)	Document Number	Booking Number
	Export References	
Consigned To	Forwarding Agent (Name and address)	
Notify Party	Point (State) of Origin or FTZ Number	
	Domestic Routing/Export Instructions	

Pre-Carriage By	Place of Receipt By Pre-Carrier	
Exporting Carrier	Port of Loading/Export	
Foreign Port of Unloading	Place of Delivery By On-Carrier	Type of Move

Marks and Numbers	Number of Packages	Description of Commodities in Schedule B Detail	Gross Weight (Kilos)	Measurement

There are: _______ pages, including attachments to this Ocean Bill of Lading

These commodities, technology or software were exported from the United States in accordance with the Export Administration Regulations. Diversion contrary to U.S. law prohibited.

Carrier has a policy against payment solicitation, or receipt of any rebate, directly or indirectly, which would be unlawful under the United States Shipping Act, 1984 as amended.

FREIGHT RATES, CHARGES, WEIGHTS AND/OR MEASUREMENTS

SUBJECT TO CORRECTION	PREPAID	COLLECT
GRAND TOTAL		

Received by Carrier for shipment by ocean vessel between port of loading and port of discharge, and for arrangement or procurement of pre-carriage from place of receipt and on-carriage to place of delivery, where stated above, the goods as specified above in apparent good order and condition unless otherwise stated. The goods to be delivered at the above mentioned port of discharge or place of delivery, whichever is applicable.

IN WITNESS WHEREOF ________ original Bills of Lading have been signed, not otherwise stated above, one of which being accomplished the others shall be void.

DATED AT

BY

Agent for the Carrier

Mo.   Day   Year

B/L No.

18. Format of Bill of Lading

There are 2 types of Bill of lading

- **Negotiable Bill of Lading**

A negotiable bill of lading is one that is delivered to a bank in the buyer's nation, signed by the shipper, and committed "to order" or "to order of shipper." Until the conditions of a documentary collection or a letter of credit are met, the bank retains the original bill of lading. Negotiable Bill of Lading are Original BL. A kind of electronic BL exists as well as a original BL. One sort of B/L that allows the carrier to release the goods to the consignee at the destination port without requiring the original B/L to be presented is a Telex Release Bill of Lading. Rather, the carrier notifies the destination agent via electronic data interchange, email, or telex of the electronic release message. Negotiable bills of lading, which offer a way to shift ownership and control of commodities while they are in transit, are crucial legal papers in international trade. They enable easy and effective trade transactions between parties participating in international trade by providing flexibility, security, and legal recognition. It facilitates the safe delivery of goods in international commerce transactions, eases the documentation procedure, and gives the shipper more control.

- **Straight Bill of Lading**

A straight bill of lading is not negotiable; it is consigned to a specific consignee. By giving the carrier an original, signed bill of lading, the consignee gives the carrier possession of the goods. Straight Bill of Lading are Seaway BL. It facilitates safe delivery of goods in international commerce transactions, eases the documentation procedure, and gives the consignee more control.

If you are working with a freight forwarder and adding a logistical partner. The MBL is a contract of carriage that is given to the goods forwarder or Non-Vessel Operating Common Carrier (NVOCC), acting as the shipper, by the ocean carrier or its agent. It acts as proof of the agreement for the shipment of goods between the shipper and the carrier. The MBL may or may not be negotiable.

The ownership of the products may be transferred by delivery of the original document and endorsement under a negotiable MBL. A non-negotiable MBL, on the other hand, is usually given when the shipper maintains ownership throughout the shipment process and does not grant ownership rights.

Upon arrival at the port of destination, the consignee or their agent must submit the original MBL to the carrier in order to take control of the cargo. The carrier releases the cargo after checking the legitimacy of the paperwork and paying any outstanding charges. The Master Bill of Lading is a basic document in international shipping that combines many shipments into a single contract of carriage between the ocean carrier and the shipper. It is essential for documenting the transportation agreement, enabling the movement of products, and settling disputes in the event of discrepancies or concerns during transit.

6. Bill of Exchange

A bill of exchange is a formal written order that is mostly used in international trade and which requires one party to give another party a certain amount of money either on demand or on a specified date. Like cheques and promissory notes, bills of exchange are drawn by individuals or banks and are typically transferred through endorsements.

<table>
<tr><td colspan="2">Bill Of Exchange</td></tr>
<tr><td></td><td>Date :
Place:</td></tr>
<tr><td colspan="2">Drawer Details :
Name:
Address:

Phone No.:
Email ID:</td></tr>
<tr><td colspan="2">Amount :</td></tr>
<tr><td colspan="2">Description:</td></tr>
<tr><td colspan="2">Drawee Details:
Name:
Address:

Phone No.:
Email ID:</td></tr>
<tr><td colspan="2">Issue Details:</td></tr>
<tr><td>Drawee seal & Signature</td><td>Drawer seal & Signature</td></tr>
</table>

19. Format of Bill of Exchange

Up to three parties may be involved in a bill of exchange transaction. The person who pays the amount shown on the bill of exchange is known as the drawee. The person who gets the amount is the payee. The person who makes the drawee pay the payee is known as the drawer. Unless the drawer transfers the bill of exchange to a third-party payee, the drawer and the payee are the same entity.

A bill of exchange, on the other hand, is a written statement of a debtor's obligation to a creditor, unlike a cheque. It's widely utilized as payment for goods and services in international trade. A bill of exchange and the accompanying forms can be used by the parties to carry out the conditions of a contract, even if it is not a contract in and of itself. It may state that money is due at a certain future date or upon demand. The term "usage" refers to the time interval between invoicing and payment. Frequently, credit terms are added to it, like 90 days. Furthermore, for a bill of exchange to be considered valid, the drawee must accept it.

Since bills of exchange typically don't pay interest, they function essentially as postdated money orders. If they are not paid by a specific date, they could accrue interest; in such case, the interest rate needs to be noted on the instrument. On the other hand, they may be transferred at a reduced price prior to the deadline for payment. The money involved, the date, and all parties including the drawer and drawee must be specified in clear and concise detail on a bill of exchange.

A bill of exchange can also be known as a bank draft if it is issued by a bank. Payment for the transaction is guaranteed by the issuing bank. Trade drafts are the term used to describe bills of exchange that are issued by private individuals. A sight draft is the term used for a bill of exchange if the money is to be paid right away or upon demand. A sight draft in international trade enables an exporter to retain ownership of the exported products until the importer accepts delivery and pays for them right away. On the other hand, it is referred to as a time draft if the money is supposed to be paid at a specific future date.

A bill of exchange differs from a promissory note in that it can bind one party to pay another party who was not involved in its production and is transferable. Promissory notes are frequently in the shape of banknotes. The creditor issues a bill of exchange directing the debtor to make a specific payment within a specified time frame. On the other hand, the promissory note is a commitment made by the debtor to pay a specific sum of money within a specified time frame.

2) Regulatory Documents

Several regulatory documents are necessary for an export business to guarantee legal compliance and promote efficient international trade operations. Major regulatory documents include IEC, RCMC, Phyto, Fumigation, COA, Shipping Bill, Export declaration, Dangerous Good declaration, and Certification Inspection.

1. IEC

The Indian government's Directorate General of Foreign Trade (DGFT) issues the 10-digit IEC identification number. It is mandatory for every individual or organization that exports products or services from India.

However, IEC will not be required for services exports unless the service provider is benefiting from the Foreign Trade Policy. IECs are issued in accordance with the PAN of the company, as a result of the implementation of GST. DGFT will still issue the IEC individually based on an application, nevertheless. Any of the following business structures may be used to get an IEC: proprietorship, partnerships, limited companies, trusts, HUFs, and societies.

2. RCMC

According to the Foreign Trade Policy (FTP), the RCMC (Registration Cum Membership Certificate) is a document that authorizes the import or export of goods that are banned. This certificate is normally issued by the Export Promotion Councils (EPCs), Commodity Boards, and Export Development Authorities that the Director General of Foreign Trade (DGFT) established for each restricted product.

An exporter dealing with products registered with an agency or organization authorized by the Indian government is validated by the Registration-Cum-Membership Certificate (RCMC). The exporter's registration with the approved agency or organization is verified by this certificate.

3. Phytosanitary Certificate

A certification that agricultural products are free of diseases, pests, and other pollutants is necessary before they may be exported. An official document called a Phytosanitary Certificate (PSC) is necessary for the export or reexport of plants, plant products, or other controlled goods. A PSC is given to confirm that the shipments comply with the specific phytosanitary import regulations of the countries of import.

4. Fumigation

A fumigation certificate verifies that all of the wood packing materials in a cargo shipment have undergone fumigation. It is also often called a pest-control certificate. Shipping cargo internationally or by sea requires a fumigation certificate. You run the possibility of your cargo not being sent, liquidated, or quarantined when it reaches other ports if you don't follow these procedures. Materials like wool, dunnages, drums, wood pallets or boxes, and other raw wood products need to be sterilized or fumigated before being shipped internationally. Nevertheless, commodities made of wood, such as cardboard, chipboard, and particleboard, are exempt.

5. Certificate of Analysis (COA)

Manufacturers provide a Certificate of Analysis (COA) as evidence to the fact that the product they made complies with the specifications provided by their customers. Customers should be sure that the product they are receiving fits their demands and that it complies with their specific goals and specifications. COAs assist your business in avoiding expensive returns, replacements, or complaints from customers.

A COA is more than just a means of product inspection. Materials must be identified and clarified accurately when they are shipped because they are moving to and from different locations quickly. The COA acts as an identity certificate for the status of each product, in addition to the labels on the materials and containers. These documents offer more specific information than what is typically seen on a label. The Certificate of Authenticity (COA) transmits data regarding the identity, quality, and purity of a particular material from the material provider to the material user. A reliable certificate of authenticity (COA) is a must for a material supplier so that the client knows exactly what kind of goods they are getting.

To find out whether the material satisfies the necessary requirements, the recipient can also check the information on the vendor's certificate of authenticity/Analysis (COA) against its specifications.

6. Shipping Bill

One crucial document that customs officials need in order to clear goods is a shipping bill. When exporting goods over international borders, an exporter must comply with a number of formalities, such as completing multiple applications, obtaining licenses, paying duties, and so forth. The "shipping bill" is the application that an exporter must submit to Customs in order to obtain a clearance for export. Until the exporter files the shipping bill, the products cannot be loaded.

An electronic shipping bill must be filed. If an electronic submission is not practical, the Commissioner or the Principal Commissioner may, however, grant an exception and accept a physical application. There are several formats for shipping bills, and they are distinguished by color.

- Dutiable Goods- Yellow Colour
- Duty-free goods- White Colour
- Goods with drawback claims- Green Colour
- Goods allowed to be exported as duty-free- Pink Colour
- Export goods under DEPB Scheme- Blue Colour

After the specific vessel, ship, etc., is permitted to leave the country and go abroad, a shipping bill can be submitted. The value of the items meant for export is determined by the customs authorities once the bill has been filed and physically checked. The customs officials check these invoices and sign both copies "LET SHIP ORDER" and "LET EXPORT ORDER." And shipments proceed and load on the vessel.

7. Export declaration

A formal document that contains details about items being exported from one country to another is called an export declaration. Authorities in the importing country may also request it, in addition to customs officials in the exporting country. A form that an exporter submits at the port of export is called an export declaration. It offers details regarding the type, number, and value of the products being sent. In addition to gathering statistical data regarding a nation's international trade, customs use this information to regulate exports. To promote trade, assure compliance with customs laws, and supply important information to governmental bodies and international organizations, export declarations play a crucial role in the export process. Exporters must become familiar with the particular requirements and protocols for filing export declarations in their country of operation.

8. Dangerous Good Declaration

The DGD's main goal is to guarantee the safe handling, delivery, and transportation of hazardous goods while reducing the possibility of mishaps, spills, or other occurrences that can endanger the environment, property, or public health. It guarantees adherence to global guidelines and norms, such as the International Maritime Dangerous Goods (IMDG) Code, that controls the transportation of hazardous materials. Carriers, freight forwarders, and other relevant authorities are notified by the DGD that hazardous items are present in the cargo, allowing them to take the necessary safety precautions and adhere to handling guidelines. Dangerous product restrictions must be followed; breaking them can have negative effects on the economy, the law, and most importantly, the safety of everyone.

To sum up, the Dangerous Goods Declaration plays a crucial role in the transportation of hazardous goods by offering crucial details that guarantee supply chain safety, compliance, and appropriate management. Collaboration between shippers, carriers, and regulatory agencies is crucial to guaranteeing the safe and secure transportation of hazardous materials.

The shipper or their designated representative must fill out and sign the DGD in compliance with all applicable laws and instructions. DGDs are frequently filed electronically using specialized hazardous materials management platforms, online portals for carriers, or electronic systems used by customs officials. Paper copies of the DGD may occasionally be needed, particularly for shipments made by rail or road, when tangible records are required for regulatory compliance or inspections.

9. Certification Inspection

A crucial commercial document needed for the import of particular consumer goods is an inspection certificate. These products could be luxury goods, electronics, hardlines, softlines, and commodities like bulk oil and scraps cargo. The inspection certificate certifies that, at the time of inspection, which is typically right before shipment, the shipment was in good condition. An essential part of transactions involving foreign trade is the document. An inspection certificate certifies that the products in the shipment have been examined by a qualified third party and have been found to comply with the terms specified in the sales agreement. It analyses to see if the products meet all requirements for quantity, quality, import eligibility, tariff classification, and cost.

These regulatory documents expedite customs clearance, guarantee product quality and legality in international trade transactions, and ensure compliance with export restrictions. To correctly prepare and submit these documents on time, exporters must have a thorough understanding of the particular criteria for their products and target markets. All of these certificates are intended for formal use at customs, If you have CHA he will take care of it. Including all other documents like a packing list, commercial invoice, and all.

• • •

CHAPTER VI

Banking

By offering a range of financial services and solutions that are specifically designed to satisfy the needs of exporters and importers, banking plays a critical role in supporting export-related activities and operations. In order to accommodate a variety of short- to medium-term trade finance requirements, streamline the entire export-import procedure, and lower the risks associated with banks' participation in trade facilitation is necessary. As a result, selecting an Bank must be decided upon after considering a number of crucial factors.

1. Current Account/EEFC Account

The Exchange Earners' Foreign Currency Account (EEFC) is a foreign currency account kept with an Authorized Dealer Category - the bank, which is a bank authorized to trade in foreign exchange. It is a feature that allows foreign exchange earners, particularly exporters, to credit 100% of their foreign exchange profits to their accounts, eliminating the need for account holders to convert foreign exchange into rupees and vice versa, hence lowering transaction costs. Individuals, businesses, and other foreign exchange earners residing in India are all eligible to open EEFC accounts. An EEFC account can only be handled as a current account. There is no interest payable on EEFC accounts. The EEFC account is eligible for a 100% credit on foreign exchange earnings, provided that the total accruals in the account for a given calendar month are converted into Rupees by the last day of the following month, after any balances have been adjusted for approved uses or forward commitments. The amount of money that can be withdrawn from an EEFC account in Rupees is also unrestricted. Nevertheless, the Rupee amount that was withdrawn is not going to be refundable to the user or convertible into another currency. Funds kept in an EEFC account can be freely transferred out of the country, paid for imports, and used to pay off foreign currency loans. Exporters may manage their foreign currency revenues and cash flows more easily and conveniently with the help of EEFC Accounts, which also help to reduce exchange rate risk.

A current account is a kind of bank account that's mainly used for business, allowing regular payments, withdrawals, and deposits.Depending on the needs of the account user, current accounts may be held in foreign currencies or Indian Rupees (INR). A current account can be used by companies who deal internationally to handle foreign exchange operations, such as paying out in foreign currencies or converting foreign currency receipts into Indian rupees. Foreign Exchange Management Act (FEMA) restrictions apply to current accounts denominated in foreign currencies, and the Reserve Bank of India (RBI) must grant permission for the account to be opened and maintained.

In summary, while managing foreign exchange transactions in India is done through both Current Accounts and EEFC Accounts, their functions differ and they are designed to meet the requirements of various account holder categories, But both can be used for the exporters. But EEFC Accounts are specialized accounts created especially for Indian exporters to maintain and manage their foreign currency profits, current accounts are general-purpose accounts used for day-to-day operations, including foreign exchange transactions.

2) How will you receive payments in USD?

After exporting goods from India, there are a few ways to get paid in US dollars (USD). The exporter and importer's preferences, the type of business relationship, and the degree of risk tolerance all play a role in the payment method selection. SWIFT Transfer is one of the most popular ways to receive international payments. The exporter gives the importer/buyer their bank account information, which includes the bank name, account number, SWIFT/BIC code, and other relevant information. The importer then initiates a wire transfer or SWIFT from their bank to the exporter's bank, indicating the payment amount in USD. And then provides a

SWIFT copy. After that, the payment will be credited to your account within 4-5 business days.

One can also use A letter of credit as a payment method which is a financial instrument issued by the importer's or buyer's bank that guarantees payment to the exporter upon presentation of certain documents and compliance with the LC's terms and conditions. The letter of credit is a secure payment instrument that provides assurance to both the exporter and the importer. Payment is provided in accordance with the Letter of credit terms once the exporter ships the products and provides the relevant paperwork (such as a commercial invoice, bill of lading, and packing list) to the importer's bank.

Online payment platforms like PayPal, Payoneer, and TransferWise allow foreign payments to be issued and received swiftly and safely. The exporter and importer can create accounts on these platforms and make USD payments directly from the importer's account to the exporter's account. Payment in USD may also be made through documentary collections. The exporter's bank serves as a middleman to obtain payment on the exporter's behalf from the importer's or buyer's bank. After the goods are shipped, the exporter ships the proof of shipment (bill of lading, for example) to their bank, which then transfers it to the importer's bank with payment instructions. Once a bill of exchange is paid or accepted, the importer's bank releases the shipping documents to the importer, enabling the importer to claim the goods. Payment in advance before delivering the products can also be the option If there are some trust issues with you and your buyer or buyer is a first time buyer, You can ask the importer to provide an advance payment. After receiving payment, the exporter can start manufacturing or exporting the goods.

All of these methods allow the exporter to get paid in US dollars. To receive and hold USD payments directly, the exporter must keep a foreign currency bank account, such as an Exchange Earners' Foreign Currency (EEFC) Account or a USD-denominated Current Account. When necessary, money can be transferred from the foreign currency account into Indian Rupees.

While deciding how to collect USD payments after exporting goods from India, exporters must evaluate transaction costs, exchange rates, payment security, and the trustworthiness of the payment process. Furthermore, exporters must follow appropriate regulatory regulations and documentation procedures for foreign payments.

3) Pre-shipment & Post-shipment Export Loan

Any finance that an exporter can obtain before shipping products to a buyer is referred to as pre-shipment finance. The exporter is required to provide the finished products as soon as a customer confirms an order. Usually, these funds are used to finance export-oriented activities including obtaining raw materials, manufacturing, packaging, and shipping. In order to meet export obligations, exporters can fulfill orders and finish manufacturing with the use of pre-shipment export finance.

Post-shipment export finance's primary objective is to give exporters short-term funding so they can handle their cash flow and liquidity issues once export transactions are completed. If finance is not available, the exporter will have to wait until the items are delivered, an invoice is raised, and the conditions of payment—which are often 30, 60, or 90 more days—come into effect. These funds are used to close the payment gap that occurs between when the goods are sent and when they are received, giving exporters the liquidity they need to meet their working capital requirements. This usually happens right before or right after the cargo is put into a ship. A number of methods, including trade loans, invoice factoring, receivables discounting, and letters of credit (LCs), can be used to provide post-shipment finance.

Pre-shipment and post-shipment export loans in India have a few main characteristics and advantages: One important aspect of loans may be their competitive interest rates. Banks and other financial institutions in India frequently offer export finance programs with attractive interest rates customized to meet exporters' needs. Flexible repayment terms, designed based on the export cycle and cash flow estimates, benefit exporters. In order to guarantee the prompt disbursement of money, banks and other financial institutions in India usually provide expedited processing of export finance applications.

Depending on the creditworthiness of the exporter and the lender's connection with them, export finance facilities can be either secured or unsecured. Collateral requirements are helpful in this case. Depending on the exporter's risk profile and the amount of funding requested, different collateral may be needed.

In order to promote export financing operations, the Indian government also supports exporters through a number of organizations, including the Reserve Bank of India (RBI) and the Export-Import Bank of India (EXIM Bank). The government may also offer banks and financial institutions refinancing options and policy support.

India's exporters may explore pre-shipment and post-shipment export funding solutions suited to their unique needs and export profiles by approaching banks, financial institutions, and specialized export credit reporting agencies. In order to efficiently fund their export activities, exporters must determine their financial needs, evaluate their options, and select the best financing arrangement. When using export finance facilities, exporters should also make sure that all applicable regulatory requirements and paperwork procedures are met. Here Banks play a very important role.

If we talk about the roles and responsibilities of banks in your exports. Banks play an important role in promoting and supporting export activity in India. Their tasks include several parts of export financing, paperwork, risk management, and advice services. Banks provide export financing options to help exporters meet their working capital requirements throughout the export cycle. This consists of pre- and post-shipment financing. Banks may offer export packing credit, export bill discounting, export finance against letters of credit, and export finance against collection bills. Banks evaluate exporters' creditworthiness, analyze the credit risk associated with export transactions, and design financing solutions based on the exporter's individual needs. Banks assist exporters prepare and process the export papers needed for customs clearance, regulatory compliance, and international trade transactions. They also offer assistance in completing export documentation such as commercial invoices, packing lists, bills of lading, certificates of origin, and export declarations to ensure accuracy and compliance with regulations. Banks also help customers comply with foreign exchange, export control, and trade finance regulations that manage transactions involving exports and foreign exchange services.

Banks also assist exporters with advising and consultancy services on a variety of international trade subjects such as market research, market trends, export strategy formulation, trade laws, and documentation requirements. Banks provide access to government schemes, incentives, and subsidies targeted at increasing exports and assisting export-oriented firms. Overall, banks play an important role in aiding Indian exporters by providing financial, consulting, and transactional services that are necessary for conducting international trade transactions and increasing export competitiveness.

• • •

CHAPTER VII

Risk Management

The goal of export risk management is not risk elimination. There is rarely a risk-free business, particularly when collaborating with clients and partners abroad. Rather, risk management entails taking action to make sure that an organization is aware of the risks it confronts, its scope, and the extent to which those risks may be mitigated. Risks associated with exporting are various. Businesses operating abroad may be subject to more significant changes in the political landscape or variations in the macroeconomic and business indicators than they would face in their home markets. Exchange rates fluctuate in value. Businesses operating in a particular nation or region may be impacted by changes to the political, legal, and business environments.

Export risks are primarily nation-specific. Some are more apparent than others, like political unrest. Establishing a solid foundation for comprehensive export risk management begins with recognizing and comprehending the scope of these threats. Exporters may strengthen their resilience, safeguard their interests, and take advantage of global trade possibilities while reducing possible setbacks and losses by taking a proactive approach to risk management. And here, we will see the strategies to reduce risk and steer clear of losses.

1) How to manage risks in Exports?

One of the challenges of exporting is learning how to deal with export risks. Identifying and managing these risks will help ensure the success of your export projects. Managing risks in exports entails recognizing possible threats to the success of your export operations and carrying out solutions to mitigate or reduce those risks.

It is possible to carry out a and Make sure you thoroughly investigate the markets you want to target and understand the legal, cultural, political, and economic aspects that could affect your exports. Also, you can evaluate the competitors, potential obstacles challenges for entry, and the demand for your goods and services. Additionally, you need to diversify your consumer base and markets to prevent being overly dependent on any one of them. Spreading your risks and lowering reliance on any one market or buyer can be achieved by diversifying your export locations and clients. If you have just one or two clients in the Middle East or the United Arab Emirates and a political issue arises, or any other unexpected circumstances occur it will completely affect and shut down your company. It will be beneficial for you to expand your clientele and grow your business if you have clients from the Middle East, the Far East, the US, and the UK. You must create thorough contracts and agreements that precisely define terms and conditions, such as payment terms, timelines for delivery, quality requirements, and dispute resolution procedures, with customers, distributors, and partners. Spend the right insurance to protect yourself against risks including currency fluctuations, unpredictable politics, loss or damage to products during transit, nonpayment by purchasers (export credit insurance), and other possible liabilities. The chapter will go into great detail about the insurance portion. With this kind of risk management instrument, your risk and your business risk factors are covered by insurance. In addition to this, you may guarantee compliance with rules. You must visit all official websites relating to trade and administration to stay informed about import/export laws, trade agreements, tariffs, and customs processes in both your own country and your target markets. Make sure you are according to the law to prevent penalties and delays to your export operations. To minimize the impact of fluctuations in exchange rates on export transactions, implement techniques to manage currency risks, such as employing future contracts or invoicing in stable currencies like the US dollar or EUR. You can also use strict quality control procedures and product testing to guarantee the reliability and security of your goods and services. Achieving or surpassing global norms and legal mandates might contribute to developing customer confidence and lowering the possibility of product-related problems or liabilities.

Additionally, as I have stated before also, create backup plans. Consider expected risks and create backup strategies to deal with them efficiently. To lessen interruptions to your supply chain or business operations, identify substitute suppliers, routes for transportation, or channels for distribution.

2) Types of Insurance

The primary goal of a business is to trade things for a profit, which cannot be achieved if the product or items that are being sold or traded are lost or stolen before being sent to their destination or destroyed during transit. Export enterprises frequently require a variety of insurance coverage to manage the risks caused by foreign commerce that is from international business/trade. Every company transaction has risks, emphasizing the significance of appropriate Import-Export Insurance plans. If your company exports, imports, or both, having the appropriate insurance coverage is critical to securing the company's long-term success. If you do not have insurance and have a bad incident during trade, transit, or production, you will be out of business, if you are a very new or bootstrap company. So insurance is necessary for safety, security, and backup. This chapter will go over the different kinds of insurance you will need for your import/export company, as well as the significance of each one in business.

1. Marine Insurance

Marine insurance is intended to secure cargo shipped by ocean. It covers risks such as vessel collisions, piracy, sinking of vessels, and other marine dangers. Businesses engaged in import/export that depend significantly on container shipping must obtain marine insurance. When booking containers for import or export, keep in mind that marine insurance is a necessary safety measure for your cargo. As the shipment moves from production to the courier's storage facilities to the selected means of transportation to the potential consumer, a lot might go wrong in the meantime and here marine insurance plays a important role in safeguarding your cargo.

2. Cargo Insurance

Cargo insurance is essential for securing your goods while in transit. Cargo insurance covers and protects your cargo from loss, damage, or theft, whether they are exported or imported. It covers all forms of transportation, including air, land, sea, and the railroad. Cargo insurance makes sure that your goods are covered financially in case of unanticipated circumstances like piracy, calamities caused by nature, or accidents. In this case, credit reports and financial data on the debtor will be provided to insurers, exporters, and importers. Following that, they will search for any unfavorable information against directors and shareholders and then report back with suggestions and support.

This insurance offers coverage for shipments made by ocean as well as other types of transport. It is regarded as one of the most complicated insurance packages since it offers insurance protection for items from the moment they get shipped from the exporter's location to the importer. This transfer process is lengthy and prone to several accidents. This insurance is the complete package of the insurance for the end-to-end coverage.

3. Export Credit Insurance

Trade credit insurance protects enterprises against nonpayment risks like export credit insurance, except it covers both domestic and foreign sales. This type of insurance coverage helps prevent a potentially hazardous scenario by providing information about the buyer's credit history and overall financial background beforehand. Small- to medium-sized enterprises and traders in particular should make use of this insurance coverage since it protects you and your company if a foreign buyer chooses not to pay you for political or commercial reasons. This insurance provides you with coverage if the overseas buyer is unable to pay for the shipment for whatever reason. You may think of it as the widely accepted yet very important policy that guarantees you won't have to let your fear of failure stop you from engaging in subsequent commercial transactions and experiencing the benefits of doing business internationally.

4. Customs Bonds and Duties Insurance

To guarantee that import/export laws are adhered to, customs officials demand a certain kind of insurance known as customs bonds. Payment of duties, taxes, and fees accurately is ensured by a customs bond. To guarantee efficient customs clearance and prevent delays or penalties, importers and exporters should get customs bonds. A customs bond is a legal contract between Customs, an importer, and a surety to guarantee that the importer will pay Customs all tariffs and fees related to import rules and regulations and other Customs-related operations.

5. Liability Insurance

To protect themselves against disputes brought by consumers using or consuming their products in other markets, exporters might additionally require product liability insurance. Liability insurance is necessary for import/export companies to protect them against disputes and other legal obligations. General liability, mistakes and omissions, and product liability are just a few of the situations that are covered by this kind of insurance. Liability insurance may assist with legal costs and compensation to victims of your exported or imported goods if they cause hurt or damage.

Domestic products are similar to international product liability insurance products. It involves the lawsuit risks and expenses that arise when proper legislation is not followed. Companies that trade with emerging countries Far East, and other Middle Eastern and African countries, many of which carry large risks but provide huge returns, are becoming increasingly popular.

6. Freight Forwarder Insurance

This type of insurance covers any liability resulting from the transportation procedure as well as loss or damage to products during transit. In the import/export industry, freight forwarders play a critical role by organizing the logistics of shipping. However, your company may suffer financial losses as a result of the errors, negligence, or carelessness of freight forwarders. In such circumstances, freight forwarder insurance covers your interests by paying for possible losses brought on by the freight forwarding company's negligence or actions.

7. Business Interruption Insurance

Your export business may suffer major economic losses as a result of disruptions. Insurance against business interruption pays for lost revenue caused by unexpected events like supply chain delays, strikes, and natural catastrophes. You can be sure that your company can bounce back and carry on after unforeseen setbacks by getting this insurance. When incidents like fires, natural disasters, or other occurrences cause delays in production or distribution, business interruption insurance covers exporters for their lost revenue and associated costs.

8. Political Risk Insurance

Exporters who want to conduct business in international markets are protected by political risk insurance from damages resulting from political events like war, civil unrest, or government and geo-political actions. Countries that employ this insurance are typically the most susceptible to interference by the government, which could lead to the loss of goods or the inability to get paid. Such governments may unintentionally pass laws that even expropriate corporate property or hinder the nation's regular financial transfer channels.

9. Currency Risk Insurance

The loss incurred by traders due to currency conversion is an important factor that can occasionally result in significant losses. You may find yourself in a state of complete despair as a result of the circumstances that existed when the transaction was started. By protecting against potential losses caused by currency fluctuations, this insurance helps. Losses resulting from changes in currency exchange rates are covered by currency risk insurance. It offers some protection against the possibility that unfavorable changes in exchange rates may hurt export transaction's profitability.

As an import/export firm owner, you must safeguard your capital, and goods and control risks. Find out more about the several insurance policies that may protect your company from monetary losses, including liability, cargo, marine, customs bond, freight forwarder, and insurance for business interruption. Having sufficient insurance coverage is essential when arranging and booking containers for import or export, as well as when negotiating container ship and freight rates.

Insurance offers protection from the unforeseen and peace of mind. To find the best insurance options for your unique business needs, speak with brokers or insurance specialists and professionals from banks and freight forwarders who have experience in the import/export sector. If you safeguard your import/export company in advance, you can concentrate on grabbing opportunities and attaining long-term success in the international marketplace. To customize coverage to their particular situation and operations, export enterprises must thoroughly evaluate their insurance needs and risks.

3) ECGC Roles and Responsibilities

The Government of India is the shareholder and operated by the Export Credit Guarantee Corporation of India Limited (ECGC). Under the Ministry of Commerce's direction, it supports Indian exporters with export credit insurance. Export Risks Insurance Corporation (ERIC) was first established by the Indian government in July 1957. In 1964, it became Export Credit and Guarantee Corporation Limited (ECGC), and in 1983, it changed its name to Export Credit Guarantee of India.

Exporters can obtain credit risk insurance from ECGC. The business handles the risks associated with importers and foreign buyers not making payments. ECGC offers banks credit insurance coverage. They support banks and manage the financing risks associated with exporters. Exporters can obtain financial institution credit facilities with the assistance of ECGC. It offers overseas investment insurance to Indian businesses that make loans or equity investments in joint ventures worldwide. The ECGC provides credit ratings and information about various countries, as well as warns exporters of potential risks associated with doing business in these countries. Furthermore, the ECGC offers information on the creditworthiness of foreign buyers. ECGC protects Indian exporters not just from credit risks, but also from the country's geopolitical and economic realities.

ECGC provides many policies, schemes, and guarantees. ECGC has divided policies into 2 parts standard and specific policies and various guarantees.

The ECGC problem focuses on providing exporters with protection against payment risk in short-term credit exports. There are four different types: contractual (comprehensive risks), contracts (political risks), and shipments (comprehensive risks) policies. Under Specific Policies, the ECGC protects exporters and Indian businesses in the event of delayed payment by insuring the export of capital goods or projects for building projects and services provided to the outside world

If we talk about the schemes provided by the ECGC, Banks offering buyer's credit insurance, line of credit insurance, overseas investment insurance, and exchange fluctuation risk insurance are covered by these schemes by ECGC.

To whom ECGC offers many promises and guarantees. And what guarantee will they provide? So, if you're doing export business, you'll require a guarantee on your business processes. Here, ECGC verifies your creditworthiness as an exporter, giving the bank confidence and faith in you to invest in your business. To protect Indian banks from potential losses, ECGC provides Financial Guarantees. If an exporter experiences payment default, ECGC handles the matter both before and after shipment. The ECGC also provides a Packing Credit Guarantee, which allows exporters to take advantage of better banker conditions. The Guarantees assure banks that ECGC will pay a sizeable portion of damages incurred in the event that the exporter is unable to fulfil its obligation to the banks. Export production Finance Guarantee assists banks in approving the full cost of manufacturing when the sum exceeds the free-on-board (FOB) threshold of agreements or orders, as well as financing needed during the pre-shipment phase. In this case, the difference stands for duty drawbacks or incentives and reward receivables. Banks typically offer exporters post-shipment financing through the purchase, negotiation, discounting, or negotiation of export bills in addition to an advance deducted from those bills. Post-shipment Credit Guarantee covers banks from foreign countries' payment-related problems, which lead to exporters' advances being unpaid. This kind of guarantee protects banks from potential nonpayment by contractors managing foreign projects when they lend money in foreign currencies.

However, several risks are not covered by ECGC; what are they? Commercial difficulties such as quality disputes, Loss caused by currency rate fluctuations, loss or damage to things that would normally be easily covered by general insurance, Situations in which exporters fail to meet or disrespect the criteria of an export agreement, If purchasers do not get import or exchange license from their respective nations if the exporter's agency or bank fails to collect money, or if commodity-related complications emerge.

To improve exporters', banks', and other stakeholders' comprehension of export credit insurance, risk management techniques, and international trade financing, ECGC also offers training courses and capacity-building programs. This gives exporters the ability to make the most of export credit insurance and guarantees and to use ECGC's services effectively.

All things taken into account, the Export Credit Guarantee Corporation (ECGC) is essential in helping India export goods since it reduces credit risk, makes financing more accessible, encourages market growth, and offers banks and exporters invaluable assistance.

4) What if Goods get Rejected?

When the quality of the goods is impaired, it is the main cause of cargo rejection. This means that the buyer will strongly refuse to accept the cargo if the exporter does not care about the material quality of the product he is exporting and it does not meet the requirements set forth by the buyer. Some customers intentionally look for reasons to not like the product's content. In this instance, you must have a total confidence in the product's quality. To prevent this kind of issue, the exporter should export his goods after providing a sample to the buyers so they may decide whether or not to buy it. There are several causes of goods being stopped at the port. Thus, what should be done if the cargo becomes stuck at port.

To prevent rejection, the seller/exporter should ask the buyer to accept the consignment at a reduced price if there is a default on the part of your side regarding the product's quality and quantity. After proposing a discount, if the buyer still won't accept the consignment, get in touch with other customers, buyers, and importers in that country to purchase the consignment at a reduced price in the same country. If you are unable to get in touch with those buyers as well, look for someone willing to purchase the cargo at any price, as it is a better than 100% loss of money. Speak with your buying agent about reselling the items in the country of destination. There are commission agents with expertise dealing in these kinds of commodities in all countries. Thus, make an effort to look for a commission agent to sell the goods in the specified country. If none of the above works for you, calculate how much freight and other costs will cost to return to your Indian factory this is called a Back To Town Procedure.

What happens if customs at the port of destination reject your products instead of the buyer? The expense to the exporter of keeping the goods in case they are refused after import customs clearance is minimal because the buyer may already have them. You could have to pay more if you decide to resell it, return it to the origin port/exporter, etc. To make up for the loss, it is recommended to persuade the same customer to accept the items and provide a discount on the next shipment.

Exporters may take more precautions, including pre-shipment inspections, more thorough quality control procedures, or more strict terms of contracts, to avoid similar problems in the future. Preventing negative events from occurring is a more straightforward approach than correcting the harm that has already occurred. Before beginning the process, find out the customs laws of the country to which you wish to send the goods. This covers general details about the place where you're shipping to or from, language restrictions, documentation needs, and products that might be illegal or troublesome in some areas. Even exporters who export frequently should periodically evaluate pertinent rules and regulations to prevent being caught off guard by unexpected changes in laws and procedures. This is because certain nations alter their import/export restrictions regularly. Overall, handling rejected items in exports necessitates careful communication, negotiation, and, in some cases, legal action to address the matter and mitigate any bad consequences for both parties engaged in the transaction.

5) What if the Buyer doesn't Make the Payment?

In an export deal, the exporter may face serious financial consequences if the buyer defaults on the payment. What therefore can the exporter do in this situation where he feels helpless? However, there are several actions you may take to ensure that you get your money recovered.

You must first get in touch with the buyer and start the conversation to find out how and when the payment is progressing. Resolving the issue through communication can often be the quickest solution when delays arise from administrative or banking processes. Remind the buyer in writing of any outstanding balance, the date it is due, and any penalties for late payment, including interest or legal action. Keep track of every communication for future reference. To settle the dispute, the seller and the buyer could negotiate, depending on the particulars at issue. This can entail talking about installment plans, delays, or other ways to pay. To obtain a clear image, you can also go to the buyer's location abroad and negotiate, ask for the money, and find out what the problem is.

The DGFT provides a more smooth process. On the DGFT website, exporters can file complaints by going to the Quality Concerns and Trade Disputes section, selecting the Services option, and uploading the necessary supporting documentation. The relevant Indian Mission Abroad (IMA) in the relevant nation is then notified of the complaint. A user guide and an online chat feature are also available on the website, in addition to a hotline with a toll-free number specifically designated for dissatisfied exporters. There is no application fee necessary for submitting a complaint under the Quality Complaints and Trade Disputes (QCTD module- The purpose of this section or module is to handle complaints or trade dispute issues whenever they emerge), and this is a free service. You can also complain, If export payments are not made on time, the buyer's credit rating may suffer. Delinquent accounts may be reported by exporters to credit agencies, which may affect the buyer's future creditworthiness. In extreme cases, You as the exporter decline to complete any more orders placed on behalf of the buyer until the final shipment's outstanding payment is collected. The buyer may feel under pressure to pay off the debt in order to keep their supply chain continuing.

If neither of these works, the Exporter can sometimes reach out to collection agencies for assistance in getting the unpaid balance collected. Collection companies are experts at chasing past-due bills, and they may employ a variety of strategies to convince the customer to send the money. Or the exporter may take legal action if negotiations and compromise don't work to fix the problem. This can involve initiating a lawsuit for breach of contract against the buyer or requesting arbitration or mediation to settle the disagreement.

If neither of these options succeeds, the seller may claim to recover the outstanding money if they have export credit insurance or other types of payment guarantees in place here you want insurance for the same in the first place. Lastly, the exporter's specific steps will be based on the situation such as the outstanding payment amount, the relationship with the buyer, and the applicable international trade laws and regulations. To protect their interests, exporters ought to carefully evaluate their choices and, if required, seek advice from lawyers.

• • •

CHAPTER VIII

Stakeholders

A company or a nation's export activities might affect or interest individuals, groups, or other entities, which are referred to as stakeholders in exports. The success of export activities depends on understanding and handling the interests and connections with various stakeholders as their involvement, cooperation, and support can have a big impact on the efficiency and results of export initiatives. In this chapter, we will look at international and Indian organizations that are involved in the export-import business and international trade.

1) International Organizations

Some problems are too huge for countries to solve alone in a world that is becoming more linked and dependent on one another. Nations have to collaborate, and one way they accomplish this is through international organizations that promote cooperation and diplomatic solutions to global challenges.

International organizations are important for importing and exporting in a globe that is becoming more interconnected day by day. Their roles encompass upholding safety standards, assisting developing countries in attaining economic stability, and setting guidelines for trade agreements and conflict resolution between countries. Understanding the role of these organizations is crucial for effective communication and adherence to import and export rules, regardless of experience level in international trade. Exporters are provided with tools, information, networking opportunities, and advocacy by multiple international organizations.

1. World Trade Organization (WTO)

The World Trade Organisation (WTO), established in 1994, is the world's largest intergovernmental economic organization. There are now 164 countries that participate in the WTO. It's headquartered in Geneva, Switzerland. The WTO's ultimate purpose and main objective is to ensure that international trade functions as efficiently, effectively, and without barriers as possible. The World Trade Organisation (WTO) is a global organization that oversees international trade rules. It serves as a forum for negotiating agreements on trade and settling disputes. It also provides resources and information to exporters.

Several World Trade Agreements have been signed by officials from member countries and approved by the corresponding legislative bodies during the organization's history. Important agreements include those aimed at creating a standard method for managing trade agreements between nations and dispute settlement procedures. The WTO serves as the forum for talks amongst its member nations.

2. World Customs Organization (WCO)

Established in 1952, the World Customs Organisation (WCO) is an intergovernmental association of customs administrations committed to the ongoing enhancement of customs procedures across the globe. Its main objective is to increase each nation's customs authority's effectiveness and efficacy to make revenue collection, trade statistic compilation, and security simpler. To promote trade and guarantee the seamless movement of products across borders, the WCO creates worldwide standards and guidelines for customs operations.

The WCO participates in the administration of WTO agreements about origin regulations and customs importance. The procedure by which customs officials place a monetary value on an item that is being imported or exported is known as customs valuation. Regulations known as "rules of origin" outline the requirements that must be fulfilled for a country to assert its claim to be the source of an item or service. When deciding whether preferential tariff treatment is applicable in a free trade zone or under the terms of a free trade agreement, rules of origin may be taken into consideration. Non-preferential rules of origin may also be implemented, for example, in order to gather trade data that is important for managing a country's economy.

3. International Chamber of Commerce (ICC)

Founded in 1919. ICC enables businesses to work together to develop standards, manage disputes, and lobby for policy change on a global scale. The International Chamber of Commerce is the world's largest commercial organization that represents private-sector interests in global commerce and trade. It provides an opportunity for businesses and other organizations to discuss and resolve issues concerning international trade.

Internationally recognized trade terms known as Incoterms are used to express precisely the costs, responsibilities, and risks that are assigned to the buyer and seller in a cross-border trade. They clarify who is in charge of making transportation arrangements, packing the products, and paying import charges. At the moment, the list of Incoterms consists of 11 terms, each of which has an abbreviation consisting of three letters (Eg- FOB, CIF, EXW etc).

4. International Maritime Organization (IMCO)

The International Maritime Organization (IMO) was formerly known as the Inter-Governmental Maritime Consultative Organisation (IMCO), which was founded in 1948. It is a United Nations specialized agency. The goal of the IMO is to establish and uphold a uniform framework for international maritime shipping, or shipping by sea, to guarantee efficiency, security, safety, and legality.

Controlling the maritime transportation of hazardous materials is one of the IMO's main responsibilities. It releases instructions on how to create an IMO Declaration for Dangerous Goods, which is a shipping document that alerts the carrier to the presence of dangerous items in a shipment and provides vital information to guarantee safe transportation.

Before a container is put onto a ship, exporters must produce a Verified Gross Mass of each container, according to a 2015 amendment. It came to light that many exporters were understating the weight of their containers, which could have resulted in safety risks. This is why the amendment was made in order to ensure

Security, Safety, Legality and efficiency.

5. United Nations Conference on Trade and Development (UNCTAD)

In 1964, the United Nations Conference on Trade and Development (UNCTAD) was founded as an intergovernmental body to help developing countries grow and strategically develop their economies. To achieve this, they removed trade-restrictive rules, expanded access to digital technology, and offered technical support, analysis, and collaboration.

A major achievement of UNCTAD is the introduction of preferential duty treatment for imports into developed nations that originate from developing countries. As a result, developing countries will be more competitive and the playing field will be more level for importers who choose to import goods from them at duty-free or at cheaper rates.

6. International Air Transport Association (IATA)

As a trade group for airlines around the world, the International Air Transport Group (IATA) was founded in 1945. The organization's objectives are to set industry standards and to assist and promote airlines. One of the main responsibilities of IATA is to control the aviation transportation of hazardous materials. It releases instructions for completing a Shipper's Declaration for Dangerous Goods, a shipping document that alerts the carrier to the presence of hazardous materials in a shipment and provides vital information for secure transportation. IATA develops guidelines and policies to ensure the safe and effective transit of freight by air. IATA's regulations assist in the efficiency of the air cargo industry, which carries out a lot of export shipping. For professionals operating in the air transport and logistics sector, particularly those engaged in exporting goods, IATA offers training courses and certificates. This makes it possible to ensure that the employees engaged in export procedures are competent and experienced in their positions.

IATA creates and advances technological advances to boost productivity and minimize expenses in air cargo operations. This includes initiatives like e-freight, which attempts to help exporters by digitizing and streamlining the documentation procedure for air cargo shipments. While IATA's major concentration is on air transport, its operations help to achieve the broader goal of promoting international trade, including exports, via air.

7. United Nations Commission on International Trade Law (UNCITRAL)

Established in 1966, UNCITRAL is an association of nations dedicated to modernizing and harmonizing regulations governing international commerce. The creation of a uniform commercial code, which offers a set of standardized guidelines for cross-border business transactions, is one of UNCITRAL's initiatives. Exporters will find it easier to do business across borders with this code in place, as it helps to maintain clarity and predictability in trade agreements. In addition to encouraging and supporting the unification of various legal systems and collecting and sharing information on case law and other legislative activity, UNCITRAL activities involve assisting states/governments of the particular country in coordinating to accomplish mutually beneficial economic goals.

To settle conflicts in international trade, UNCITRAL encourages the use of alternative dispute resolution procedures like mediation and arbitration. UNCITRAL guarantees a swift settlement of disputes and assists exporters in reducing the risks connected with international trade by offering frameworks and regulations for these procedures.

8. International Organization for Standardization (ISO)

Representatives of national standards organizations from all over the world comprise the International Organisation for Standardisation (ISO), which was established in 1947. Its goal is to establish and uphold global standards to guarantee the effectiveness, fairness, and safety of trade across borders. ISO maintains standards in a wide range of industries, including manufacturing, transportation, energy, healthcare, agriculture, financial services, and information technology. It is not industry-specific.

Logistics, traceability, and sustainability are just a few of the elements of supply chain management that are covered by ISO standards. Ensuring supply chain accountability, effectiveness, and sustainability through compliance with ISO standards boosts exporters' trustworthiness and quality. The ISO certification serves as proof that a business's operations, goods, or services fulfill global requirements for efficiency, quality, and safety. Customers and commercial partners can feel reassured by accredited certification bodies that use audits and evaluations to determine compliance with ISO standards.

ISO standards are essential for promoting uniformity, quality, and compliance along the whole supply chain, which helps to facilitate exports and trade globally. Understanding ISO standards helps exporters become more competitive, builds confidence between trading partners, and promotes long-term economic growth.

International organizations are essential in helping exporters because they offer trade promotion services, financial support, advocacy for policies, capacity-building initiatives, understanding of markets, and legal advice. Exporters can increase their global business possibilities and manage the challenges of international trade by interacting with these organizations.

2) Indian Organizations

The provision of several forms of support, guidance, and resources to enterprises by Indian agencies is a critical factor in helping and promoting exports. These organizations serve as facilitators for the promotion of Indian products and services in foreign markets as well as in India and the management of the challenges associated with international trade. The following is a list of councils for commodities exported from India. And without their facilities, licensing, and promoters, exporting cannot be done smoothly. The export of different commodities from India is greatly aided by export promotion councils, boards and agencies. These councils and boards are sector-specific groups set up to encourage and assist the export of particular goods or areas. They offer exporters a variety of services, such as policy advocacy, capacity building, market intelligence, and networking opportunities. We know that export licensing is an important part of international trade, and numerous councils, boards, and agencies in India issue licences, authorizations, permits, and certifications that promote exports.

- A List of Indian councils that promote exports of a certain commodity:-

1. Apparel Export Promotion Council (AEPC)
2. Chemicals, Cosmetics & Dyes Export Promotion Council (CHEMEXCIL)
3. Carpet Export Promotion Council (CEPC)
4. Cashew Export Promotion Council of India(CEPC)
5. Council for Leather Exports (CLE)
6. Electronics and Computer Software Export Promotion Council (ESC)
7. Engineering Exports and Promotion Council (EEPC) India
8. Export Promotion Council for EOUs & SEZs (EPCES)
9. Export Promotion Council for Handicrafts (EPCH)
10. Gem & Jewellery Export Promotion Council (GJEPC)
11. Indian Oilseed and Produce Export Promotion Council (IOPEPC)
12. Jute Products Development & Export Promotion Council (JPDEPC)
13. Mobile and Electronic Devices Export Promotion Council (MEDEPC)
14. Pharmaceuticals Export Promotion Council of India (Pharmexcil)
15. Powerloom Development & Export Promotion Council (PDEXCIL)
16. Sports Goods Export Promotion Council (SGEPC)
17. Cotton Textiles Export Promotion Council (TEXPROCIL)

18. The Indian Silk Export Promotion Council
19. Plastics Export Promotion Council (PLEXCONCIL
20. Synthetic & Rayon Textiles Export Promotion Council (SRTEPC)
21. Wool & Woollens Export Promotion Council (WWEPC)

- A list of Boards Promoting other commodities are:-

1. Food Safety and Standards Authority of India (FSSAI)
2. Tea Board
3. Tabacco Board
4. COIR Board
5. Species Board
6. Marine Products Export Development Authority
7. Rubber Board
8. Coffee Board
9. Coconut Development Board
10. Agricultural and Processed Food Products Export Development Authority (APEDA)
11. Other important boards are EIC, RBI, and BIS.

- Trade Regulating Agencies:-

1. Central Board of Indirect Taxes and Customs

Indirect tax administration, customs duty collection, and the upholding of Indian customs regulations fall within the authority of CBIC. It falls under the Ministry of Finance's Department of Revenue. Customs laws and regulations about the import and export of products into and out of India are enforced by CBIC. It guarantees adherence to trade laws, tariffs, and customs processes to support lawful commerce and deter illicit activity like smuggling and customs duty evasion. With the implementation of modern technology for customs clearing procedures, the simplification of documentation requirements, and the streamlining of customs procedures, CBIC plays a critical role in trade facilitation. It seeks to lower transaction costs, boost productivity, and encourage importers' and exporter's ease of doing business. The CBIC is in charge of managing the administration of indirect taxes, including the Goods and Services Tax (GST), which took the place of the prior system of state-level taxes, central excise charges, and service taxes. To help the government fund its operations, it creates policies, carries out tax legislation, and collects indirect taxes. Enforcing customs laws and regulations is the responsibility of CBIC in order to stop criminal trade operations, such as smuggling, trafficking in counterfeit goods, and avoiding customs duties. It carries out audits, investigations, and enforcement procedures to make sure customs regulations are followed and to discourage breaking them.

CBIC improves the understanding of customs rules, processes, and compliance requirements among importers, exporters, and customs officials, CBIC organizes workshops, seminars, and training programs. It encourages skill development and professional advancement in customs administration. Overall, the Central Board of Indirect Taxes and Customs is essential to the regulation of global trade, revenue collection, compliance assurance, and facilitation of legal trade activities in India. Its operations are critical to safeguarding national interests, fostering economic expansion, and preserving the integrity of the customs system.

2. Directorate General of Foreign Trade (DGFT)

One important government organization in India that is in responsible for developing and carrying out foreign trade policies, encouraging exports, and overseeing foreign trade operations is the Directorate General of Foreign Trade (DGFT). The Foreign Trade Policy (FTP) of India was developed by DGFT. It outlines the government's approach and goals for increasing exports, boosting competitiveness, and expediting trade. The FTP is often updated to reflect shifting domestic economic interests and the realities of international trade. The DGFT's goal is to encourage exports from

India by giving exporters a range of advantages, incentives, and support programs. It is responsible for managing various export promotion programs, including Duty-Free Import Authorization (DFIA), Advance Authorizations, Export Promotion Capital Goods (EPCG) scheme, Merchandise Exports from India Scheme (MEIS), and Services Exports from India Scheme (SEIS). For export-import activities, such as importer-exporter code (IEC) registration, export licenses, duty drawback claims, and export obligation discharge certifications, DGFT issues licenses, permits, and authorizations. It controls international trade and guarantees adherence to export-import guidelines. To promote Indian products and services overseas, network with potential customers, and investigate export prospects, DGFT arranges trade shows, seminars, exhibitions, and trade missions. To facilitate customs clearance and ensure compliance with export rules, DGFT offers exporters advice and support in creating export documentation, including shipping bills, export declarations, certificates of origin, and other export-related documents.

In short, the Directorate General of Foreign Trade is essential for encouraging exports, managing international trade, and assisting with transactions across borders. Its activities are crucial for increasing market access, making Indian exporters more competitive, and promoting economic development.

These export promotion councils, boards, and agencies are essential for supporting exporters and ensuring that export operations for their particular commodities are carried out efficiently. They support India's export industry's expansion and competitiveness in international markets with their efforts and services. To ensure the efficient issue of licenses and permits for exports, cooperation between government agencies, trade associations, and industry organizations is essential. Exporters must keep up with industry-specific regulations and work with the appropriate agencies to get the licenses and certificates required to carry out export operations legally.

3) MOC, MEA, MOF, Customs

These acronyms refer to different Indian government departments and agencies that deal with commerce, finance, and international affairs.

1. MOC- Ministry of Commerce and Industry

To support economic growth and development, trade and industrial policies must be developed and put into action by the Ministry of Commerce and Industry. It is responsible for all things about foreign investment, trade both domestically and internationally, industrial development, and intellectual property rights.

2. MEA- Ministry of External Affairs

The Ministry of External Affairs is in charge of managing India's diplomatic and international affairs. It negotiates treaties and accords, oversees diplomatic posts overseas, represents India in international organizations, and offers consular services to Indian nationals living outside.

3. MOF- Ministry of Finance

Managing the country's financial and economic issues falls within the responsibility of the Ministry of Finance. It creates and carries out fiscal policies, which include financial rules, taxation, budgeting, and public spending. The ministry is also in charge of capital markets, insurance, and banking in India.

4. Indian Customs

The government organization responsible for controlling the flow of products into and out of the country is known as Customs. The Central Board of Indirect Taxes and Customs (CBIC) in India is in charge of managing customs activities. Enforcement of customs rules, collection of duties and tariffs, prevention of smuggling and illicit trade, and facilitation of lawful trade through adherence to import and export regulations are all performed by customs authorities.

These government agencies and departments are essential to the development of India's trade policies, the management of foreign relations, and the maintenance of customs compliance necessary for trade and commerce to run effectively.

• • •

116

CHAPTER IX

Government Schemes

Governments provide schemes to export businesses for several reasons, main among them being to encourage and support export growth, which is essential to a nation's economic success. Government export business initiatives are essential for boosting industrial development, employment creation, economic growth, and national interests in international trade.

1) Major Promotion Schemes for exports

The Government of India has implemented two important schemes, RoDTEP (Remission of Duties and Taxes on Exported Products) and DBK (Duty Drawback Scheme), to encourage exports and offer exporters different advantages. The government's main promotional strategy is to offer tax reductions. So, what are those schemes?

1. Remission of Duties and Taxes on Exported Products (RoDTEP)

To pay back exporters for the tariffs and taxes they paid when exporting goods, the Indian government launched the RoDTEP scheme to replace the Merchandise Exports from India Scheme (MEIS). By returning the embedded taxes and fees, RoDTEP aims to increase the competitiveness of Indian exports on the international stage while lessening the disadvantage that Indian exporters suffer from the non-refund of these charges. RoDTEP Schemes include an extensive range of levies and taxes that are not reimbursed under the present scheme, such as central excise fees, state taxes, municipal levies, and customs duties. The RoDTEP rates for various products and businesses that export are established by analyzing data particular to the industry. The program efforts to give Indian exporters fair and equal opportunities in the global market and is made by the rules of the WTO. RoDTEP regulates both commodities produced domestically and goods imported for export.

2. Duty Drawback Scheme (DBK)

DBK is an existing mechanism that refunds customs charges paid on imported inputs used to create exported goods. Exporters can utilize this scheme to request a refund of customs charges paid on raw materials, components, and intermediates used in the production of exported goods. The DBK intends to reduce the impact of customs charges on exporter's production costs while also making Indian exports more competitive in foreign markets. The DBK rates are determined using the duties paid on the inputs used in the production of the exported goods. The plan includes both basic customs charges and extra levies, such as anti-dumping and safeguard duties levied upon imported goods. The Directorate of Drawback, Ministry of Finance, Government of India, provides DBK rates, which are routinely updated to reflect changes in input prices and other variables. DBK is available for exporters from a wide range of sectors and is an important source of export incentives for Indian businesses.

The purposes of DBK and RoDTEP are the same: to support exporters by returning duties and taxes paid during the export process, to encourage exports, and to increase the competitiveness of Indian products in international markets.

2) Transport and Marketing Assistance (TMA)

The Indian government launched the Transport and Marketing Assistance (TMA) scheme for agricultural products. It seeks to provide less expensive freight- a term used to describe the transportation of goods- which is a crucial component of modern international trade. This program has reduced the cost of transportation needed to export a few particular agricultural products. To make our agricultural products competitive in the worldwide market, it means that the government will refund the freight costs up to a certain amount. Additionally, it offers advantages for agricultural product marketing, supporting brand promotion, and helping to establish Indian agricultural products awareness in international markets. All exporters with eligible agricultural products who are registered with the relevant Export Promotion Council by the Foreign Trade Policy are covered by the scheme. The exporter's portion of the freight (air and sea) and marketing expenses related to product promotion are to be reimbursed under the transport and marketing support program.

Inshort, The main objective of Transport and Marketing Assistance (TMA) is to assist with the international freight component and the sale of agricultural products. TMA also mitigates the disadvantage of increased transportation costs for exports of specific agricultural products due to transshipment. They also promote brand recognition for Indian agricultural products in the designated international markets. Assistance under the TMA scheme is calculated by taking into account the FOB (Free on Board) value of exports as well as the notified rates that apply to certain items and export destinations. All things taken into account, by offering financial support to offset high transportation and marketing costs, the Transport and Marketing Assistance (TMA) scheme plays a critical role in supporting exporters of agricultural products and specific goods, thereby enhancing their ability to compete while encouraging export growth from India.

3. Infrastructure Projects and Initiatives of Government of India to Increas Exports.

The Indian government has been aggressively executing a number of infrastructure projects with the objective of increasing the country's export capacity. These initiatives are critical because they contribute to reduced trade costs, improved connectivity, and increased global competitiveness of Indian goods. In this part, we will look at the numerous initiatives and infrastructure undertaken by the Indian government to improve and increase exports.

1. Sagarmala Project

Port modernization, new port construction, improving port connection, and coastal community development are the main objectives of this expansive programme. Sagarmala's primary objective is to lower the cost of logistics for both domestic and export-import goods. This initiative's projects include the creation of many coastal economic zones, which should greatly increase exports. New ports are being built, such as the transhipment port at Andhaman, the Vadhvan Port in Maharashtra, and the Ramayyapatnam Port in Andra Pradesh. These ports will undoubtedly boost our exports while lowering the logistical costs of connecting to the East, West, North, and South.

2. Bharatmala Project

This road and highways initiative, which is government-sponsored and supported, intends to improve road connectivity throughout the nation with an emphasis on maximizing the effectiveness of freight and passenger movement. To cut down on the time and expense involved in moving goods from manufacturers to ports, Bharatmala will link India's main production and consuming hubs.

Phase I of the NHDP saw the construction of approximately 34,800 km (21,600 mi) of highways, comprising 24,800 km (15,400 mi) of new highways and an additional 10,000 km (6,200 mi) of ongoing work that is still unfinished due to many issues like labor strikes and shortage, Funds, Politics, and Land acquisition, etc. This is in contrast to the 19 years that the NHDP required to upgrade nearly the same length of National Highways. These roads are part of the National Corridors Efficiency Programme and feature 6-8 lane, bypass, and ring roads for 6 NC. 3,300 km of border roads and 2,000 km of border and international connection roads link six national corridors to international commerce routes, including Bangladesh-India-Nepal (BIN), MIT, and BIMSTEC. In many Indian cities, multimodal logistics parks are also being developed. It will increase the efficiency of the current corridors, enhance communication with the northeast, and capitalize on the interplay with inland waterways. In a hub-and-spoke configuration, multimodal logistics parks will facilitate smooth cargo movement between railroads, inland waterways, air cargo, dedicated freight corridors, access-controlled motorways, national highways, and state highways.

3. Dedicated Freight Corridors

These are railway tracks with great speed and capacity that are intended only for freight. The most well-known dedicated freight corridors are the Eastern and Western ones. They are designed to relieve traffic on traditional routes, shorten freight transit times, and increase the effectiveness of freight transportation along the vital east-west and north-south corridors for trade.

The Eastern and Western freight corridors are the two lengthy routes that the Ministry of Railways started constructing as part of a new Dedicated Freight Corridor (DFC). The two routes have a combined length of 3,260 kilometers: the Western Dedicated Freight Corridor runs from Jawaharlal Nehru Port in Mumbai, Maharashtra, to Dadri in Uttar Pradesh, and the Eastern Dedicated Freight Corridor runs from Ludhiana, Punjab, to Dankuni, West Bengal. The project's primary objectives are to upgrade transportation technologies, boost productivity, and lower unit transportation costs.

4. Corridors for Industrial and Heavy Goods

Many industrial corridors are being developed by the government across the country, such as the Amritsar-Kolkata Industrial Corridor (AKIC), the Chennai-Bengaluru Industrial Corridor (CBIC), and the Delhi-Mumbai Industrial Corridor (DMIC). The transportation of goods will be made easier and more affordable with the integration of smart cities, industrial clusters, and efficient road, rail, and port infrastructure that these corridors are expected to feature.

5. Development of Inland Waterways

The government's goal with the Jal Marg Vikas Project is to expand inland waterways, especially National Waterway-1 (the Ganga River between Varanasi and Haldia), to facilitate transportation via inland water. This offers a feasible, economical, and logistically efficient way to move goods—especially big goods—while also clearing traffic on the roads and rail systems.

Through these and other projects, India hopes to establish a holistic ecosystem in which logistics costs are reduced and production is increased, hence enhancing the competitiveness of

Indian goods in the global market. This is consistent with India's overall goal of becoming a more major role in the global trading system.

Exporters should stay up to date on the government's latest announcements and scheme modifications. This can help you maximize the benefits. The exporter has to understand the compliance standards. Each scheme has its own set of compliance criteria. Exporters should ensure that they understand these regulations to prevent losing potential benefits due to non-compliance. Exporters ought to look for professional assistance. Given the complexities of the schemes, getting legal representation from export promotion consultants or professionals can help you navigate the export promotion landscape effectively.

• • •

CHAPTER X

Packaging

An important factor in determining a product's apparent value is its packaging. In addition to aiding in the administration and display of the product, they also include, safeguarding, and taking care of it. The importance of packaging has to be demonstrated in organizations entire marketing efforts. A high-quality and beautiful package helps the audience recognize the product inside in a positive light, earns customer trust, and undoubtedly influences purchasing decisions. Just like the Parle product, You can recognise it anytime you see yellow color packet with a small girl on biscuit pack.

Designing and producing packaging is the process of wrapping or covering a product to ensure protection, ease of handling, and storage. Packages can be designed for ease of distribution, management, display, selling, opening, use, and recycling.A distinctive package allows a product to stand out. Colors, shapes, pictures, and other elements can create distinctive and original packaging.

However, this is about marketing and distribution in the end. But during export transit, excellent export packaging ensures that your valued goods arrive safely and intact. Assume that the goods left from your side without proper export packaging and were damaged during transit by ship or transportation, and your customer refused to accept your item, the result would be a loss-loss situation. Export packaging is the outermost layer of packing that protects products in transit, and it includes both internal packaging and products. It is primarily used by organisations delivering high-value, sensitive or delicate machinery or expensive commodities that must remain in excellent condition while in route/transit.

1. Packaging Types

Packaging for export is determined by a variety of criteria, including the nature of the items being shipped, their fragility, destination country restrictions, and cost concerns. Shipping standards vary throughout countries, states, and provinces because packages are most usually handled by a network of conveyors and cranes. With this in mind, the type of transportation item must be examined based on weight, size, and commodity.

Items that are heavy (or ordered in quantity) may necessitate more durable packing to ensure their safety, whereas equipment or vehicles require specialized transport and export packaging. Which includes many packaging types like Boxes, Pallets, Crates, Drums/ Barrels, Flexi-bags Packaging, Small Container, Loose packaging etc.

Shippers worldwide use boxes and cartes for international shipping. Boxes and crates are used to pack various products. Both may be made from wood, but their structures differ. Packaging boxes are sturdy and covered on all sides to keep goods safe. Crates, on the other hand, may have open sides with a solid top and bottom (making items easier to see for quick inspections). They are versatile, affordable, and provide adequate protection for a wide range of products. Corrugated boxes come in a variety of sizes and can be customized to meet the specifications of the products being delivered. Wooden crates are durable and offer good protection for heavy or fragile products. They are frequently used for transporting machinery, equipment, and heavy items.

Pallets are often used for export packaging. They are a flat transport structure that supports and stabilises goods when they are lifted by forklifts or cranes. Pallets serve as the structural underlying for a load unit, dividing shipping container products into discrete units. Items placed on pallets are typically tied with straps or shrink wrap for increased security. Pallets are used for stacking and transporting large products. They are frequently used with shrink wrap or stretch film to keep the products in place. Palletized shipping is effective for transporting large amounts of items and is widely utilized in industries such as manufacturing, retail, and agricultural products.

Drums/Barrels are typically used for transporting liquids or powders that must remain dry. Drums can be constructed from a range of materials, including fibre, stainless steel, and polyethylene. These are utilised for transporting liquids, chemicals, and other items that need to be kept secure. Plastic drums are lightweight, resilient, and corrosion-resistant, making them ideal for long-distance transportation.

Others like small container or cardboard packaged boxes are used for stationery products, fruits etc. And loose pacaking is done for large cars or machines may not be enclosed and are transported as general shipping instead. Dunnage or other protective materials are used to fasten objects and prevent moisture absorption (which can cause corrosion). The sender of shipping items is responsible for ensuring that their goods are secure and securely in place in ship/vessel. This can also be classified as specialised packaging. This specialised packaging is dependent on the nature of the goods, and it may be required. This could include temperature-controlled packaging for perishable things, anti-static packaging for electronics, pharmaceuticals, and medicines, as well as hazardous materials packaging for chemicals and dangerous commodities.

Foil packaging is also used as a export packing to reduce the risk of corrosion during transit. These can be customized to fit a wide range of freight requirements. Equipment is foil-wrapped, with desiccant added before the final seal. Air is removed, lowering ambient moisture levels and reducing bulk size.

Flexi-bags, also known as bulk bags or large bags, are used to carry and store dry bulk materials including grains, powders, and granules. They are comprised of woven polypropylene fabric and can contain a big amount of products while offering some protection against moisture and contamination.

When choosing suitable packaging for exports, consider the mode of transportation, handling requirements, destination restrictions, protection, security, cost, wood packaging, and the particular needs of the goods being exported. Furthermore, ensuring that the packing meets international norms and regulations can assist avoid delays and ensure a seamless export procedure.

2. Packaging Cost

Packaging costs in the export business can vary greatly based on a number of factors, including the type of product being exported, its fragility, destination, shipping method, and specific packaging requirements specified by international regulations or the importer's preferences. When considering packaging expenses in an export business, it's important to account for items like as boxes, crates, pallets, cushioning materials (e.g. bubble wrap, foam), tapes, labels, and more. You can consider design and customization of both the inside and outside of the product as a cost of packaging cost. As If the packaging needs to be customized to fit the product or fulfill special branding requirements, there may be extra design, printing, or branding expenses. This packing protects against shock, vibration, heat, moisture, and dust as per commodity properties. Packaging combines small products into a single box for efficiency and cost reasons. For example, storing 1000 pencils in a single box rather than 1000 pencils in individual boxes is preferable. The same applies to clothing, shoes, and other things. The cost of manpower and transportation can also be considered. Labour costs include the wages of packing workers who assemble, fill, seal, label, and prepare goods for transportation. Labour charges varies depending on the size, quantity and weight of the goods. The same holds true for transportation costs. Transportation costs associated with bringing packing materials to the manufacturing plant or warehouse where the items are prepared for export. The handling and storage of goods Specific handling or storage needs for packaged items, such as temperature control or particular handling operations, may increase overall packaging costs. Compliance and certification costs should also be considered when calculating packing costs. Some products may require additional certifications or compliance with international packaging regulations, which could increase the entire cost. And insurance for the same must be purchased to protect the packaged items during transit from damage or loss. The cost of insurance might vary depending on the value and nature of the products. Some products, such as medications, perishable goods, food, or sensitive goods, and hazardous goods, are rejected by the buyer if the packaging is damaged. Which could be a loss that can be reimbursed through insurance. Consideration of regulatory standards might be expensive. Different countries have different regulations for packaging materials, labeling, and documentation. Ensuring compliance with these regulations may necessitate additional resources and costs. Environmental considerations are a key packaging cost when exporting. Sustainable packaging options are becoming increasingly important. Using eco-friendly materials or implementing recycling activities may increase expenses, but they can also provide long-term benefits. Consider currency exchange and tariffs when offering a final quote to your buyer. Because if you do not consider this, fluctuations in currency exchange rates and tariffs on imported packaging materials can influence prices, particularly if packaging materials must be exported.

Exporters must carefully consider these variables and establish a complete packaging strategy that balances cost-effectiveness with meeting the needs and expectations of customers and regulatory agencies in their target countries. Furthermore, investing in high-quality packaging can help protect items in transit and improve the overall brand image. Proper packaging and labelling not only improves the appearance of the end product, but it also saves money by protecting the product from being mishandled during the export process and maintaining the overall image of the brand, service, and protection.

3. Sample Packaging

If a buyer asks for a sample to be sent with your export shipment, make sure the sample is properly packaged to demonstrate the quality of your goods and avoid any damage in transit.

First select packaging materials that offer suitable protection for the sample while it is being shipped. This could include foam inserts, bubble wrap, strong cardboard boxes, or any other protective materials appropriate for the particulars of the sample. Warp the sample to protect the sample from vibrations and shocks during shipment, carefully cover it in foam or bubble wrap. Make sure the sample is sufficiently covered and safeguarded on all sides. For the same, you can use your inner package. To give more protection, consider utilizing additional inside packaging if the sample is sensitive or delicate. To stop movement within the outer packaging, this could involve putting the sample in a smaller box that is filled with crumpled paper or packing peanuts/foam. Additionally, if you are creating inner packaging, remember to clearly mark the sample. How will the buyer know that this is the sample that the seller/exporter sent? The product name, description, quantity, and any other pertinent information should all be visible on the label of the sample package. Upon acceptance, this will make it easier for the recipient to identify the sample. Add any other supporting materials that are required, such as a product specification sheet or an overview of the sample's characteristics and advantages. This will give the recipient important details regarding the sample. When clearing through customs at the port, this can also be helpful if there is an open examination. Using sturdy and robust packing tape, firmly seal the outside package to prevent the sample from moisture and damage while in transit. Verify again all of the gaps and openings are properly sealed to minimise the possibility of the package opening in shipment in transit. Additionally, take care when inserting the packaged sample into the export shipment package. Make sure it is firmly in place and enclosed in the proper materials to keep it from moving or becoming damaged by any other items in the package. Add the buyer's information, the delivery address, and any other relevant details on the export consignment package label. State on the label that there is a sample included in the package for simple identification, and make sure the buyer knows about the identification mark on it. Inform the buyer as soon as the package is ready and ready to ship, give any relevant tracking information, and ensure that the sample was included. Instruct them to get in touch if they have any queries or worries regarding the shipment.

By appropriately following the above procedure, packing, and providing a sample with the relevant details. To create a favorable image of your business and increase the buyer's trust in your items, make sure the sample is packaged carefully and expertly.

4. Packaging Institutes

There are various packaging institutes and organisations in India that focus on the research, creation, instruction, and promotion of packaging technologies and techniques for both domestic and export markets. There are numerous packaging courses available both online and on campus.

IIP is an autonomous organisation that reports to the Ministry of Commerce and Industry in India. Located in several cities such as Delhi, Kolkata, Chennai, Hyderabad, and Bengaluru. It provides a variety of courses, consulting services, testing facilities, and research and development in packaging technology.

The Central Institute of Plastics Engineering & Technology (CIPET) is headquartered in Chennai and has locations throughout India. CIPET is a top national institution run by the Department of Chemicals and Petrochemicals, Ministry of Chemicals and Fertilisers, Government of India. It provides teaching, training, research, and consulting services in the field of plastics engineering and technology, particularly packaging.

Other organisations include the Indian Flexible Packaging & Folding Carton Manufacturers Association (IFCA), which is based in Mumbai. The IFCA is an association that represents India's flexible packaging and folding carton sector. It encourages industry growth, technological advancement, and best practices in packaging.

The Packaging Association of India (PAI), based in Mumbai. It is a non-profit organisation dedicated to the promotion of packaging industry experts in India. It offers a forum for networking, knowledge sharing, and advocacy on packaging-related concerns.

The Indian Institute of Packaging Technology and Research (IIPT&R) is located in Hyderabad. IIPT&R is a private institution that provides education, research, and consulting services in packaging technology and research. The Indian Institute of Packaging and Food Processing (IIPFP) is located in New Delhi. It is a research and educational organisation that provides a variety of courses and training programmes in the packaging and food processing industries.

This is the institute where you can learn and get trained about packaging and build your packaging operation for export. You also have the option of giving it to a third party. There are numerous packaging companies that specialise in packaging and related services. They customize packaging to meet your requirements and deliver it to you. However, there is a high cost involved. And one cannot accept the risk of packaging high-quality stuff for third-party packing. It is better to do it yourself. What if the third-party packing company fails to include a key element or component in the box or consignment, or includes any other material not listed in the list? Your shipment may be rejected by the buyer or detained by a customs official. Consider third-party packaging at your own risk, and learn about the packaging company's past and expertise.

• • •

CHAPTER XI

Marketing Analysis

Starting an export firm requires a thorough market analysis. This comprised various variables, such as product and market selection, as well as the overall market, which included both the global and domestic markets. It will assist you in clearly defining your export objectives, such as target markets, products/services to export, desired growth rates, and timetables. It will also assist you with competitive analysis, primary research for regulatory and compliance requirements, market entry plans, risk assessment, financial analysis, and so on. By taking these steps and completing thorough market analysis, you will be able to make informed judgements and design a successful export business strategy that maximises potential while minimising risks in target markets.

1) Product Selection

Starting an export business in India without a specific product in mind can be a tough but rewarding endeavour. Selecting the right product to export from India is similar to selecting the perfect recipe for a delicious dinner or purchasing the appropriate suit for your prom night. It's a decision that can lead to new opportunities and advancements. India, with its blend of traditions and diverse products, has several options for exporters. But making the right decision is critical, and it may make or ruin your export business. Starting an export business in India without a specific product in mind can be a challenging yet exciting endeavor.

Understanding what you are unable to export is equally as vital as understanding what you can. A list of goods that are prohibited or restricted from being exported from India is maintained by the government. On its website, the Directorate General of Foreign Trade (DGFT) maintains an up-to-date list of them. Apart from these goods, the decision of what to export essentially rests with you.

It is a good idea to find a product category or service that makes you desire to export. Maybe there's a certain product that stimulates your interest, or perhaps you want to export a product that hasn't yet made it "Good or mainstream"—for me, that was a pharmaceutical item—what interests you? Either way, you have some preliminary homework to complete. Selecting a product at random and attempting to sell it abroad is not a wise business move. Similar to this, even when a product stimulates your exporter-entrepreneur spirit, it might not be in demand overseas, which could be disastrous for your company.

What factors, then, may you use to select your export product? Learning how to select the best product for your export company requires giving serious thought to several different factors.

1. Market Research

Conduct extensive market research to uncover products that are in great demand globally but may not be readily available or cost-effective for production in India. Look for new trends, specialized markets, or items with a distinct value proposition. What are the most well-known products from India? How about your state? What are its main exports? Who imports from us? Find solutions to every basic inquiry you can think of. Examine the historical trends and patterns of our nation's exports, as well as those of your state. The majority of this data is available in open databases maintained by the Ministry of Commerce and the DGFT. You may determine what we sell well and which of our products have a solid reputation abroad by looking at India's trade data.

2. Identify exportable products and evaluate the supply and demand for them on the global marketplace

Think about goods that India produces more cheaply than other countries. Textiles, handicrafts, spices, agricultural products, engineering products, pharmaceuticals, and software services could all fall under this category. Assess these products' export potential in light of variables such as demand in the intended countries, competitive pricing, and product quality. After considering this you will learn more about the product and its supply chain, including how it is made, where it gets its raw materials from, who makes it, what components it has, whether it is seasonal, how much demand there is for it, whether you can meet it, how to market it, whether you can provide guarantees or replacements, etc. The inquiries that you must make will differ depending on the goods. Finding out how much demand there is for the product, if you can meet it, and how long it will take are some of the most crucial facts to know.

3. Do Networking

Participate in exhibits and trade shows, Attend trade shows and exhibitions across the globe to learn about a variety of items and make connections with producers, distributors, and business specialists. Such events can offer insightful information about new trends and export prospects. Establishing a network among exporters, suppliers, trade associations, and governmental organisations participating in global commerce. They may offer insightful advice, market data, and prospective product leads.

4. Evaluate Regulatory and Compliance Requirements

Do extensive study on the regulatory and compliance requirements for exporting to other nations before finalising any product. Ensure that the product of choice conforms to all applicable international norms and laws. Regarding trade laws and compliances, each market is unique. You should be fully informed of the laws in the country where your goods is being shipped. Find out if the country of destination has a history of limiting similar products or imposing high import taxes and levies. You ought to become knowledgeable with the nation's commercial ties to India as well.

5. Think About Infrastructure and Logistics

Evaluate the exporting of your selected product in terms of its infrastructure, including storage, transit, packing, and customs clearance. Think about goods with low logistical hurdles and ease of transportation.

6. Evaluate Profitability

Consider variables such manufacturing costs, market demand, competition, and possible profit margins as you examine the profitability of exporting various goods. It is advisable for businesses to select products that hold the potential to yield financial rewards. In addition to making sure your target market is prepared to pay a fair price for the goods, you also need to determine where the product is produced most cheaply. It would also be a good idea to see how the product has performed over time. Determine whether it is prone to periodic or seasonal tendencies. Estimate all product-related costs, including those for shipping, taxes, and tariffs, and compare your profit margin to the sale price.

7. Start modest

To test the waters and get experience in international trading, consider beginning with a modest product line or niche market. As you gain experience and establish your place in the international market, you can gradually extend your product line. Unless your product and/or offering is unique, you are likely to face tough competition from businesses that are currently exporting similar products from within your geographic area. In this instance, you must show your product as unique and distinguishable from your competition. Your product's unique selling point could be superior quality, a lower price, better after-sales service, or a mix of these and other aspects. A word of caution when competing on priceing merely lowering your pricing may succeed briefly, but it will eventually reduce your own profitability. You may require a different long-term USP. Once you've decided on the product you want to export, you should limit the markets to which you can ship it, as well as look into the numerous incentives and benefits available for trading it.

8. Seek Expert Advice and Be Confident

If you're not sure which products to export, speak with export consultants, trade advisors, or industry specialists. They can offer significant insights and advice based on their experience and skill in international trade. Be certain that you can accomplish it and that the product quality you can give is the greatest in the market, as client retention is crucial in exporting. And if you don't believe in your product, the consumer will.

This is how you can select your product. Remember that creating a successful export business involves patience, perseverance, and the willingness to adapt to changing market conditions. be up to current on market trends, regulatory changes, and emerging possibilities to be competitive in the global marketplace. Selecting the appropriate product is critical for export success. It entails deciding what the world wants while also focusing on your strengths. This decision has the potential to lead to financial success, long-term stability, and international expansion.

2) Market Selections

One of the most critical factors in international marketing is market selection. Expanding into overseas markets can provide huge growth prospects for firms. However, choosing the appropriate export markets necessitates considerable consideration and strategic decision-making. Not all markets are equally ideal for every organization; considerations such as market size, competition, cultural fit, and regulatory environment must all be taken into consideration. Here you can find all of the important aspects for analysing and selecting the best overseas markets for export expansion.

1. Size and Potential of the Market & Growth

Start by researching possible markets for your goods. Take into account variables including market demand, rivalry, the regulatory landscape, cultural variances, and economic stability. It is critical to evaluate the target market's size and growth potential. Greater sales and expansion prospects could be presented by a wider market. Finding markets with strong growth potential and demand for the goods or services being provided can be facilitated by analyzing market trends, demographics, and economic data. Seek for markets that have a strong economy and a substantial consumer base. Rapid growth potential might be found in emerging areas, yet stability and greater purchasing power might be found in established markets.

2. Competitive Ecosystem

It's essential to comprehend the competitive landscape. Assess the degree of rivalry within the intended market, the hegemony of current participants, and the obstacles to entry. Determine what makes your company stand out from the competition by analysing their advantages and disadvantages. Finding untapped markets or market gaps might provide you a competitive edge.

3. Cultural Fit and Market Entry

Successful market entry requires cultural compatibility. Analyze the target market's cultural values, tastes, and habits. Think about how well your goods and services fit the preferences, customs, and way of life of the locals in the particular market of that country. Marketing tactics, product attributes, and messaging can be modified to better fit the local culture to increase acceptability and customer involvement. Cultural differences may affect how overseas markets view your items. To understand customer preferences, behaviour, and business etiquette in your target markets, conduct cultural research.

4. Assess the Regulatory Environment

Know what is required for you in terms of regulations to export your goods to other nations. Import taxes or other stringent laws in some regions could have an impact on your company. Understand the target market's trade policies and regulatory requirements. Consider elements including laws, certifications, intellectual property protection, and import restrictions. Examine any possible obstacles or limitations that might affect market entry and continuing business operations. Adherence to regional laws is necessary to prevent legal issues and guarantee a seamless export procedure.

5. Identify Distribution and Logistics Channels

Take these factors into account when choosing markets. Consider elements like distribution network accessibility, infrastructure, and shipping costs. Examine the distribution channels suitability and availability in the intended market. Evaluate the effectiveness of the current logistics infrastructure, distribution networks, and transportation systems. Think about the advantages of forming local presences through subsidiaries or partnerships or forming agreements with local distributors.

6. Risk Assessment

Evaluate the target market's risks in great detail. Analyse potential trade obstacles, currency volatility, economic concerns, and political stability. Doing due diligence, feasibility studies, and market research can help determine the viability and possible dangers of entering a particular market.

7. Monitoring and Adaptation

After selecting a market, regularly monitor and analyse its performance. Adapt strategy in response to market input, customer behaviour, and changing market dynamics. Be willing to change your marketing strategies, distribution networks, and product offers in order to stay competitive and responsive to the needs of your target market.

8. Get Professional Assistance

Consider contacting trade associations, export promotion councils, or government bodies that offer exporters support and direction. They can provide useful information, market insights, and networking possibilities.

You can choose the best markets to start your export business in India by carefully considering all of these factors and completing extensive market research. Remember to constantly monitor market conditions and adjust your plans to maximize your chances of success.

3) Source of International Market Analysis

Listed websites that can provide information on international trade data, market research for your export items, voluntary standards in place, particularly in large developed markets and retail chains, investment flow and opportunities, and so on.

1. Trade Map:- www.trademap.org/Index

An online application that provides monthly, quarterly, and yearly international trade data, as well as statistical indicators and trading company information, to assist you in prioritising export or import markets.

2. Market Access Map:- www.macmap.org

An online tool for analyzing global market access circumstances, including applicable and binding tariff rates, trade agreements (rules of origin and tariff preferences), export-import statistics, and non-tariff measures.

3. Standards Map:- www.standardsmap.org/standards_intro.

An online tool for analysing and comparing voluntary standards encouraging sustainable development in the production and distribution of goods and services.

4. Investment Map:- www.investmentmap.org/home

An online tool that gives sector-specific information on foreign direct investment (FDI), trade, market access, and foreign affiliates to help with investment attraction and targeting strategies.

Using these tools and techniques, as well as doing a thorough market study, you may find prospective export possibilities and establish successful plans for entering and succeeding in international markets from India. Consider consulting with trade specialists, industry associations, export promotion councils, and government agencies to promote your export goals.

• • •

CHAPTER XII

Company Formation

Starting an export company in India requires multiple procedures and considerations. Starting an export company in India requires many steps and considerations. Export firms are broadly grouped into three types: manufacturing-export units, export traders, and service-export units. Manufacturing export units produce goods and products for international markets. Export traders serve as merchants, exporting domestically created commodities to foreign countries. Service export units operate to supply services to international customers. So first find you are in find your company in which group.

1. Company Registration

After choosing group and make a business structure then determine the regulatory structure of your export company- Sole Proprietorship Partnership, Limited Liability Partnership (LLP), Private Limited Company (PLC), Public Limited Company (listed or unlisted. For small businesses or partnerships, a sole proprietorship or limited liability partnership (LLP) is preferable. You need to do the company registrations via government portal. Choosing suitable company types is important. The firm owner or partners must select the most appropriate business structure. Choosing the wrong business structure can have a huge impact on the finances of both individuals and businesses, as each business structure has various compliance requirements. Similar to auditing Registering a corporation legally allows for an accurate audit of its accounts and ledger. To guarantee that this is done in accordance with the rules, business stakeholders must hire auditors and have numerous accountants on the payroll. As a result, if you adopt an improper business structure, these expenses can reduce the company's revenue. Income Tax: As stated in the above structures, the business's tax on the income received by its stakeholders differs. A company must file both its income tax return and its tax return with the registrar of companies, whereas a sole proprietor only needs to file their individual income tax return. Business Expansion affects this, Since various business types impose restrictions on business expansion, it is essential to select the appropriate business structure. Certain companies have the ability to draw in more investment due to their greater investor-friendliness.

2. All Licenses- IEC, RCMC, Port Registrations

In India, registering a company is now simpler than ever. Whether you are looking for information on how to register a private limited company or any other type of business structure, all you need to know is the four basic components that you should focus on. The company registration process is now done online, which makes it easier to use and more efficient.

IEC code/certification is essential. Individuals or businesses engaged in import and export activity in India must obtain an IEC. It is issued by the DGFT. You can apply for an IEC online via the DGFT website.

RCMC is issed by Export Promotion Councils (EPCs) or Commodity Boards. It is essential to receive numerous perks and incentives under various export promotion programs. Depending on the nature of your export operation, you may require RCMC from the appropriate EPC or Commodity Board.

Port registrations and its registration code may be necessary based on the ports you intend to export from. Every port may have its own registration processes and requirements. This registration supports the seamless processing and handling of cargo at ports.

Export Licence for Specific Products are essential for some products. Certain products may require specific export licences or permissions due to regulatory requirements. Agricultural items, chemicals, pharmaceuticals, and some types of machinery, for example, may be subject to further regulatory licencing or permissions.

GST Registration is also important. If your export turnover exceeds the threshold limit, you must register under the Goods and Services Tax (GST) system. GST registration allows you to receive refunds for taxes paid on inputs used in the process of exporting.

Quality certificates are needed depending on the nature of your commodities, you may need to obtain quality certificates or meet specific quality standards set by countries that import them. For example, ISO certification, CE labelling, or specialised product certifications may be required.

Do we need certification for customs clearance? Yes.If you intend to manage customs clearance processes yourself, you may need to obtain a Customs Clearing Agent Licence. Alternatively, you can hire a licenced customs clearing agent (CHA) to conduct the clearance on your behalf.

Other Regulatory clearances and approval certificate may also need. Depending on the industry and type of items you export, you may be required to seek other regulatory clearances or licences from appropriate authorities. Environmental clearances, phytosanitary certificates, and health and safety certifications may all be required.

It is essential that you thoroughly analyse the precise standards governing your export operation and verify compliance with all applicable laws and regulations. Consulting with legal and trade specialists can help you successfully manage the licensing and registration process.

• • •

CHAPTER XIII

Marketing

Marketing is essential to export business's success for a number of reasons. Export companies can expand their consumer base and access international markets with the use of marketing. They can also assist you with market expansion. Marketing activities such as promotion, branding, and advertising campaigns assist exporters create reputations and trustworthiness in international markets, which will help you build your brand. Exporters can effectively position their products in foreign markets by using marketing to showcase features, benefits, and USPs of their products/goods that appeal to international buyers. Exporters can stand out in crowded markets and draw in target clients with the aid of effective product positioning. However, in order to stand out in your marketing, you must first understand certain basic approaches and ideas. And in this chapter, we'll look at which techniques and strategies are best for you as a beginner exporter.

1) Marketing your Products & Company

Before starting an export sales plan, an exporter should have particular goals and thoroughly research the markets. With the use of an export sale/marketing plan, businesses may easily design a blueprint for selling their goods overseas. Without a defined strategy for navigating international markets, a corporation may find it challenging to succeed. Building a business and developing a marketing plan is crucial when launching an export enterprise. Similar to other organizations, import-export businesses need greater understanding when they deal with international customers. After mastering export marketing management in this chapter, you can quickly succeed in business by developing an effective marketing plan. So, starting with the basics, what is marketing strategy? In simple terms, a marketing strategy is a collection of activities that you carry out to make your product stand out in the marketplace. If your marketing strategy is good, your sales will be good.

In the export industry, traditional marketing may not be highly popular, but it gives you an advantage over rivals who don't use it. During the 1970s and 1980s, marketing strategies made use of word-of-mouth, billboards, commercials, and other forms of advertising a lot. By participating in or going to foreign trade shows, you may leverage this method to build relationships with buyers and professionals on a one-on-one basis. However, after the 1990s, television and, later, the Internet came. Creating an internet presence is the finest way to export online marketing. Making a website is not the only marketing approach; alternatives include social media ads, email marketing, content marketing, SEO (Search Engine Optimisation), and many more. Online marketing makes it easy for the customer to learn about the company or the product. You can carry out a niche marketing plan by utilizing SEO and internet digital marketing strategies. It works incredibly well for both novices and experts. By choosing your audience's age, behavior, location, and interests, you may target them using niche marketing. You can research your target market and then market your goods according to their preferences. By doing this, you might increase your chances of making the sale.

Take a note that "COST" is an important consideration in the export business for both the exporter and the buyer. So you can also do cost marketing. Cost marketing is a type of marketing strategy that employs discounts, bulk pricing, promotions, and memberships to attract buyers who are interested in your products. Cost marketing is one of the most effective marketing strategies. Everyone enjoys saving money, and if you provide such a solution and standout option for buyer than your rival, you will undoubtedly receive orders. Cost marketing is effective for domestic customers as well.

The most significant aspects include customer service and after-sales support. Provide great customer service and after-sales assistance to keep customers satisfied and loyal. Respond quickly to inquiries, answer customer problems, and ensure order delivery on schedule to promote confidence and goodwill in overseas markets which will lead to word of mouth and help you get future leads. In addition, a continuous evaluation and adaption procedure involving consumer reviews and technology should be followed frequently. Regularly monitor and analyze your export marketing efforts to identify opportunities for enhancement and adaptation. To be successful in the global marketplace, one must be adaptable and responsive to changes in market dynamics, consumer preferences, and the competitive environment.

By using a systematic approach to export marketing and adhering to all of these instructions from Traditional Marketing to After Scales Support, you can successfully market your company's goods internationally and attain long-term success and growth in the export industry.

2) Creating a Product Catalog

Catalogues are powerful instruments that let you connect with your international customers and distinctively showcase your business. They are more than just marketing materials. To make sure your product catalog properly presents your offerings to potential buyers, export businesses must go through several phases in the creation process. Before launching a catalog without a clear aim, objective, or structure, decide what your catalog's purpose is and compile all the product details you'll need, including composition, measurements, cost, and feedback from customers. After that, organize and analyse the layout of your catalog, taking into account elements like product details, categories, and visual design. Next, use tools and templates to construct your catalog, emphasizing the special qualities and advantages of your products. Lastly, make your catalog available online or download it so that it can be printed and distributed. By following the below steps, you will be well on your way to creating a professional-looking catalog for your export company that effectively communicates your point of view to a buyer residing outside of India.

1. Determine Who Your Audience Is:- Identify your target market, such as distributors, retailers, and wholesalers based in another country. Recognize their wants, preferences, and areas of difficulty and how you are solving their issue and needs.

2. Establish your Objectives for Your Catalogue:- Select the format for your catalog (online, printed booklet, digital PDF, etc.). Take into account your target audience's ease of dissemination and accessibility.

3. Gather the Content for Your Catalogue:- Outlining is essential while making a catalog. Before you start designing, gather and organize your content from the front cover to the back. Images, products, services, corporate information, testimonials, a table of contents, and contact information should all be included in your material. A well-structured outline guarantees that every aspect matches your intended objective, making it easier to manage your catalog's material, such as a good front cover, introduction page, table of contents, main content, and final pages. Guide on how to order and contact you, including your email address, phone number, and address on the back cover.

4. Highlight that your product is export-friendly:- Highlight features that qualify your items for export, such as conformity with international standards (ISO, CE), multilingual packaging, and adaptability to various climates or conditions.

5. Provide Specific Product Details:- Provide technical details, specifications, and thorough product descriptions in several languages. Any certificates, guarantees, or quality assurances that are important to buyers worldwide should be made clear without getting confused.

6. Include Foreign Exchange and Currency Conversion (If needed INR to USD):- Provide costs in many currencies to satisfy customers from around the world. Provide precise terms and conditions about the cost, exchange rates, and available payment options so there will be no misunderstanding or problem in the future.

7. Feedback from Valuable Customers:- Include case studies, endorsements, or recommendations from satisfied customers abroad to build credibility and confidence. To show that you have expertise servicing to international markets, highlight your successful export collaborations or initiatives.

8. Also Address Rules and Regulations for Exports from India:- Clarify shipping alternatives, delivery times, document requirements, and associated fees for foreign orders. Provide details about packing requirements, customs clearance processes, and any import and export regulations that buyers should be aware of.

9. Personalise for different markets:- Customise areas of your catalog to meet the specific needs and preferences of various export marketplaces for customers based in different nations across the world. Consider adjusting product dimensions, packaging, or features to fit cultural or regulatory variances.

10. Utilise Digital and Printed Formats:- Provide print and digital copies of your catalog to accommodate varying tastes and media channels to reach your target market audience. Make sure the digital copies can be downloaded or shared with ease and are optimized for internet viewing.

11. Put Feedback Mechanisms in Place:- Invite foreign buyers to provide comments so that you may keep improving your catalog's ability to satisfy their wants. Update the catalog frequently to take into account modifications to the product line, industry developments, or legal specifications. To move forward, get expert feedback by asking them for their opinions. Include all of your website's information and feedback. For this, you will need a website. So, get one website for your business to make yourself visible on the internet, and keep your business details updated regularly we will see in the next chapter how to create a website for an export business.

12. Promote Through All Export Channels:- Distribute your catalog via internet marketplaces, trade groups, international trade exhibitions, and export promotion organizations. To reach potential customers worldwide, make use of digital marketing techniques like email campaigns and social media advertising.

By following these steps and customizing your strategy to the particular needs of export markets, you can develop an extensive and successful product catalog that draws in foreign customers and promotes the expansion of your export company. Although making a catalog could appear challenging at first, with careful planning and attention to the above-mentioned processes, you can produce a captivating and powerful marketing tool that draws in clients and increases sales.

3) Website for Export Business

Professional Appeal builds trust with potential foreign customers and strengthens company credibility. This is necessary for market expansion. makes it easier to enter new markets, increasing the potential revenue and consumer base. Reaching your target consumer and increasing your exposure in search engine results are made possible by SEO optimization, which also draws more visitors from your target export markets. Localized content offers a customized experience for viewers around the world by supporting numerous languages and currencies. To guarantee compatibility across a range of devices and increase user engagement and conversion rates, responsive design is also crucial. and Integrated Analytics for the consumer study. supporting data-driven business decisions by offering insightful information on the behavior of users across the globe.

Obtaining your export company website will provide you with this polished appearance. Your company's and product's marketing includes SEO, content, and other elements. However, where will you advertise? And if you don't have a website, where your customers may cross-check your business's existence. They cannot travel the entire globe to only confirm the existence of your business. They can ensure that you are real and not a fraud if your website is updated with every detail are in place.

So what should be added to your website?

1. Homepage with About Us:- We discuss our experience, mission, and the ideals that underpin our approach to global trade.

Don't forget to introduce your export firm and highlight its major components on your homepage, such as the products or services you provide, your target markets, and any unique selling factors. Share the story of your export firm, including its background, goals, values, and team members.

2. Products or Services you offer Page:-Include thorough information about the products or services you offer for export. Include high-quality photos, specifications, and pricing details. A complete summary of the export services you provide, such as logistics, documentation, and compliance. Add a portfolio of your exported items, including specs, categories, and industries covered.

3. Contact Us Page:- Get in touch with our staff to begin a new export project or with any questions. Make it simple for prospective customers to contact you by providing a phone number, email address, physical location, and other contact details and social media page links.

4. Add Testimonials on Homepage:- Include client endorsements or case studies that showcase your accomplishments in exporting goods. To win back the trust of previous clients, it's a very smart marketing move to include success stories and testimonials from customers who have profited from our export solutions.

5. Add FAQs:- Create a list of frequently asked questions concerning your export company that prospective customers may have, and clearly address each one. Frequently Asked Questions (FAQs) assist buyers in finding immediate responses to frequently asked questions about exporting your products.

6. Add Industry News & Blog Links:- Articles on trade news, expert interviews, advice, and best practices for the export sector may be found on our blog. Additionally, distribute updates about your company, relevant industry news, or informative sources about the goods or services you export.

7. Other Relevant Details:- If you're targeting international markets, you can think about including language and currency options to make your online presence more accessible to a worldwide audience. You can also include information on shipping choices, delivery times, and any applicable shipping policies or restrictions. Add your conditions of service, the policy on privacy, and any other legal terms relevant to your export business. Ensure that your website is compatible with mobile devices, since many potential clients may access it via smartphones or tablets. Additionally, link your website to your social media profiles and encourage people to follow you for updates and promotions for social interaction.

To create a website for your export business, you can use free website builders that include customizable themes and user-friendly interfaces. If you want your website to be more visually appealing, you can employ developers to create and manage it. As an alternative, you might hire a web developer to create a custom website that meets your needs and analyzes the data for you.

4) Online/Offline Marketing Techniques

To reach a wide range of buyers and increase your market presence, export businesses might use a combination of online and offline marketing strategies.

For organic traffic online, make sure you have a nice website and your website is search engine (SEO) optimized, responsive to mobile devices, and user-friendly. To determine a website's ranking for a specific keyword, search engines such as Google and Bing consider more than 200 + factors. If you follow these factors, That means more than 36% of your target audience will find you when you rank better for a specific term in organic results.

So, focus on on-site SEO factors and guidelines when creating your import-export website. Add content that is rich and good in keywords. Also, try to reduce the time it takes for pages to load on the website. A bot-friendly sitemap should also be added. Create informative content about your business or products, such as blog data entries, articles, infographics, and videos. This pulls in new clients and establishes your expertise. It goes without saying that your goal as an exporter of goods or services is to draw in buyers from all over the world. You may be interested in finding out how popular your goods or services are in different target countries. You can learn more about the searcher's purpose by conducting a comprehensive keyword analysis. When customers are searching for the goods or services your company offers online, you can get in touch with them. Thus, content marketing with the right keywords can enable you to generate quality leads.

If you don't have active profiles on multiple social media platforms, you are losing out on almost all prospective buyers/ importers globally. Social media ranks postings according to the number of likes, hearts, and comments you receive, allowing businesses to showcase themselves immediately on user feeds and attract more site visitors.

Develop company accounts on social media sites such as Facebook, Instagram, and Pinterest to advertise export services with attractive deals. Use social media sites like Facebook, Instagram, LinkedIn, and Twitter to interact with your followers, give updates, and promote your merchandise.

To keep your audience informed and engaged, create an email list and send them newsletters, promotions, and product updates. Additionally, to target particular demographics or geographical areas, spend money on pay-per-click advertising campaigns on social media channels or platforms like Google Ads and do PPC Advertising.

You can also collaborate with influencers in your industry or niche to market your goods to your audiences. You can also place your goods on online marketplaces such as Amazon, eBay, Alibaba, or Etsy to reach a larger audience. Since COVID-19, when all operations were closed, the online marketplace and online events have there going on. Even webinars and online events were boosted to attract more buyers. People host webinars, workshops, or virtual trade shows that can be used to educate and engage potential consumers.

If we talk about offline marketing for export businesses, attracting offline buyers can take different shapes, such as going to trade exhibitions, building connections and links with associations for the industry, and making use of personal networks.

You can attend trade shows for offline marketing. You can also set up a booth at a trade show can be a great opportunity to network with potential consumers and promote the products you sell. Search for trade exhibitions in your target markets and sectors. The list of exhibitors and visitors can be found on the websites of your most likely prospects. Look for regular international trade shows and exhibitions that are relevant to your product, both in your own country and the country you are targeting. Try to visit them, or at the very least obtain the exhibitor and visitor database.

You can also become a member of industry associations to network with prospective customers and remain informed about news and developments in the industry. Participate in conferences and networking activities organized by these associations. Additionally, you can take part in government trade programs. Trade initiatives are provided by numerous countries and can assist companies in reaching out to prospective customers and entering new markets. Look for programs administered by your government or the government of your target market.

You can also use traditional marketing channels for offline marketing. Offline, traditional methods of marketing like direct mail and print advertising can still be useful for attracting potential customers. Think about sending selected buyers direct mail or running advertisements in trade magazines. Additionally, giving away samples of your goods is a great approach to spark interest and develop a connection with possible customers. Consider hiring local agents to assist you in interacting with potential buyers, selling your products, and providing free samples in your target areas.

Remember that developing connections, networking, and establishing trust are essential for successful exporting. Be flexible, persistent, and willing to explore new options. Combining these online and offline marketing tactics allows you to develop an integrated plan for promoting your export business and attracting customers from all over the world.

In the end, marketing increases sales, increases market share, and boosts customer lifetime value to boost revenue growth and profitability for export companies. Exporters can increase their return on investment, achieve sustainable growth, and succeed in global markets by investing in efficient marketing techniques and ideas.

• • •

CHAPTER XIV

Experience, Experts and Seminars

1) Exporter Experiences from the Past

One of the primary reasons for the failure of many exporters, who quit after a few months of effort, is that they lack business blueprints. They don't receive advice from professionals. They just concentrate on the sales portion of the business rather than concentrating on learning as much as they can, networking, comprehending the psychology of the client, and using force marketing to raise the company's profile.

They don't value their company's online presence, and last but not least, they lack a methodical approach to working step-by-step to receive export orders.

Over the years, Indian exporters have built up a lot of knowledge negotiating a variety of obstacles and grabbing opportunities in the global marketplace. Indian exporters are now aware of how important it is to uphold strict quality standards and adhere to global laws and norms from their past. To guarantee that their products are accepted in international marketplaces and to establish enduring trust with clients, they invest in quality control methods, certifications, and compliance processes.

Indian exporters have a firsthand understanding of the difficulties associated with supply chain management and logistics in global trade. They now know how to minimize risks related to transportation, customs clearance, and warehousing, as well as optimize shipping routes and inventory management.

Exporters have experienced difficulties due to currency fluctuations, terms of payment, and availability of credit. They developed tactics for controlling currency risks, negotiating favorable payment terms, and leveraging financial tools such as insurance for export credit and trade financing facilities to reduce financial risks.

Exporters have gained knowledge about international distribution networks and tactics for entering into unfamiliar and new markets. To penetrate new markets and increase their clientele, they have investigated a variety of strategies, including direct exports, partnerships, joint ventures, and e-commerce platforms.

Indian exporters have insight into the particulars of export-import laws, paperwork specifications, and trade restrictions in various regions. To prevent delays and penalties, they have learned how to deal with regulatory obstacles, secure the required licenses and permissions, and guarantee compliance with trade regulations. Indian exporters have understood how important it is to differentiate their products in cutthroat international marketplaces through brand creation and marketing. To increase their brand exposure and market presence, they make use of digital marketing methods, take part in trade events and exhibits, and cultivate long-lasting connections with buyers.

Exporters have proven to be adaptive and strong in the face of obstacles like trade disputes, geopolitical unrest, and economic downturns. To adapt to shifting business conditions, they have learned to innovate, diversify into new product categories or markets, and reposition their strategies. Exporters and new exporters appreciate the Indian government's support through export promotion initiatives, promotions, schemes and trade facilitation measures. They regularly work with government agencies and industry associations to advocate for policies that encourage export growth and reduce trade barriers.

Indian exporters continue to play an important role in promoting export growth, increasing competitiveness, and contributing to India's global economic development by using their previous experiences and lessons learned. If you want to start a business and are having trouble figuring out how to start an export business or have any business-related questions, the best thing you can do is meet with experienced exporters in that field, freight forwarders, and CHA and discuss your problems and solutions.

It's important to remember that exporting has additional challenges, such as managing logistics, understanding foreign laws, and cultural differences. However, companies may successfully take advantage of exporting's advantages and increase their brand awareness in the international market with the right preparation, market research, and strategic alliances.

2) CHA

Customs House Agents (CHAs) help importers and exporters with customs clearance procedures and documentation requirements, which is a critical part of their function in promoting international trade. A CHA's main task is to facilitate trader's documentation at customs. They serve as liaisons between customs officers and the traders they represent, helping to finalize the necessary paperwork and guarantee smooth operations. They are also in charge of making sure the cargo arrives on time. They are in charge of processing carriages or vessels and approving transports for the inward and outward movement of various carriers, such as railroads, vessels, and air.

A CHA is also responsible for auditing the import and export of goods at the customs station. A CHA in export is frequently misidentified as a freight forwarder. A freight forwarding agent's main responsibilities include managing logistics and transportation of exports. They also manage the entire export procedure, including the route and mode of shipment. However, shipping CHAs can help you with the intricate processes well in advance of the export. They will understand the terms and conditions since they have the necessary information on ground process at port as well.

For CHAs to conduct trade legally, they must seek a license from the Central Board of Indirect Taxes and Customs (CBIC in India). A license can only be obtained by fulfilling specific requirements, including maintaining financial stability, being a competent professional, and following rules and guidelines.

- What function do CHAs perform, then?

CHAs help their clients clear customs by preparing and submitting import/export paperwork on their behalf. This entails submitting shipping invoices, bills of entry, customs declarations, and any other necessary documentation needed for customs evaluation and clearance. To facilitate the effective and seamless transfer of goods across borders, CHAs collaborate with a range of parties involved in the import/export process, such as shipping agents, goods forwarders, customs officers, and other service providers. In customs-related concerns, such as customs inspections, audits, assessments, and dispute resolution procedures, CHAs advocate for their clients, protecting their rights and ensuring procedural compliance.

- How is CHA selected for your exports?

CHA's Accuracy. On behalf of their clients, CHAs are in charge of making sure that all documentation and customs declarations are accurate and comprehensive. CHA must be doing documentation and process timeliness. To prevent delays and penalties, CHAs must follow the specified schedules and dates for filing customs declarations, making duty and tax payments, and following the steps involved in the customs clearance process. He must wants to keep everything confidential. To comply with privacy and data protection laws, CHAs must handle sensitive client information and trade-related data with integrity and confidentiality.

In overall, Customs House Agents (CHAs) are essential to the effective movement of commodities across international borders and the success of international trade transactions because they make customs clearance procedures for importers and exporters easier and more compliant. Keep an eye out for a few things when searching for a CHA in shipping. This comprises experience in the appropriate field and domain knowledge. We are aware of how confusing documentation and procedures may be for exporters and traders, particularly those attempting to export for the first time. Here CHA will assist you for smooth process.

3) Freight Forwarders Meet

Forwarding companies may showcase their services, meet potential customers, and gain knowledge about the newest developments in the sector by participating in trade events and exhibits that concentrate on logistics, transportation, and supply chain management. Examples of seminars are the CII Logistics Conclave, in India, the International Federation of Freight Forwarders Associations (FIATA, India, Transport Logistics in Munich, Germany, and Intermodal Europe in Amsterdam, Netherlands. Freight forwarders can meet possible partners, collaborators, and clients at networking events hosted by chambers of commerce, business organizations, and professional organizations. Business luncheons, breakfasts, and evening receptions are a few examples of these gatherings where people can network and exchange business cards. Since freight forwarders are the target audience for these seminars and meetings, why should exporters attend?

Attending freight forwarders meetings can be quite beneficial for Indian exporters for several reasons.

1. Networking Opportunities

Exporters can network with a variety of industry specialists at freight forwarders meetings, including customs brokers, freight forwarders, logistics service providers, and transport operators. Developing a connection with these stakeholders may open up fresh opportunities for collaboration, partnerships, and enterprises.

2. Business Development

Exporters can present their goods, services, and skills to prospective clients and partners during freight forwarders meetings. Exporters can create leads, land new contracts, and expand their clientele by taking part in trade exhibitions, networking events, and business matching programs.

3. Meet Experts

Presentations, panel discussions, and workshops given by thought leaders and industry experts are common features of freight forwarders meetings. By learning about emerging technology, industry trends, best practices, and regulatory changes, exporters can improve their knowledge and skills in international trade.

4. Market Analysis and Regulatory Compliances

Exporters can obtain market information and remain up to date on supply chain trends, market prospects, and the dynamics of global commerce by attending freight forwarders meetings. Exporters can use this data to analyze consumer preferences, identify new markets, and create focused export plans. Seminars on trade documentation, customs procedures, and regulatory compliance may be included in meetings for freight forwarders. Exporters can more effectively negotiate the difficulties of international trade by gaining a greater awareness of export-import regulations, tariff classifications, and documentation requirements.

5. Problem Solving and Collaboration

In international trade, exporters frequently encounter challenges and bottlenecks such as delays in customs clearance, problems with transportation, and red tape. Exporters can address these issues with industry colleagues and freight forwarding professionals at freight forwarders' meetings. They can also get guidance and look into working together to find solutions to common difficulties.

By participating in freight forwarders meetings in India, exporters can gain invaluable experience in networking, learning, collaboration, and business growth within the dynamic and competitive realm of international trade.

- List of Freight Forwarding Meetings and Seminars:-

1. India Warehousing and Logistics Show (IWLS)
2. India International Logistics Expo (IILE)
3. CII Logistics Conclave
4. Customs Brokers and Freight Forwarders Federation of India (CBFFI) Conferences
5. Global Logistics Summit (GLS)

6. Cargo Connect
7. JC Trans Meetings
8. FNC Meetings
9. India Freight Awards
10. International Federation of Freight Forwarders Associations (FIATA) World Congress

4) Export-Import seminars

Exporters, importers, and professionals involved in international trade can all benefit from the insights, knowledge, and networking possibilities that export-import seminars provide. A wide range of subjects about laws, market trends, export-import procedures, and best practices are covered in the seminars. Here are some export-import seminars that exporters may want to attend, followed by a list of these seminars.

1. International Trade Seminars

Many aspects of international trade are covered in these seminars, such as logistics, import and export documentation, customs compliance, and financing of trade. To help exporters and importers deal with the challenges of international trade, they offer useful guidance and suggestions.

2. Export Complaint Workshops and Seminars

To make sure that importers and exporters follow all relevant rules and regulations, compliance workshops concentrate on regulatory requirements, export controls, sanctions, and trade compliance procedures. To improve their understanding of compliance issues, they might incorporate interactive workshops, case studies, and compliance training.

3. Market Entry and Export Strategy Seminars

To help exporters find new markets, evaluate market prospects, and create successful export plans, these seminars examine market entrance tactics, market research methodologies, and export planning frameworks. Topics including branding, product adaption for foreign markets, and export marketing might also be covered.

4. Export Promotion Scheme Workshops

These workshops include details about government programs for export promotion, incentives, and benefits that are accessible to exporters. Some of the programs covered by these workshops include duty drawback, export credit, and export incentives under MEIS (Merchandise Exports from India Scheme). They assist exporters in comprehending the standards for eligibility, application processes, and compliance to take advantage of export incentives.

5. Customs and Trade Facilitation Seminars

Customs clearance techniques, tariff classification, valuation regulations, and trade facilitation strategies to simplify import-export procedures and lower trade barriers are the main topics of customs seminars. Additionally, topics like free trade agreements, preferential trade agreements, and customs risk management might be covered.

6. International Trade Law Seminars

Contracts, Incoterms, dispute resolution processes, and international trade law frameworks like WTO agreements are among the topics covered in these seminars on the legal elements of international trade. They give importers and exporters knowledge of legal concerns and risk-reduction tactics related to international trade.

7. Trade Credit and Loan Financing Seminars

To facilitate export transactions and control financial risks, financing seminars concentrate on export finance options, trade credit insurance, letters of credit, and export credit guarantees. They offer information about how to reduce payment risks in international trade and obtain funding for expanding exports.

8. Industry-Specific Exports-Import Seminars

Industry-specific seminars cover the requirements of importers and exporters in various industries, including electronics, manufacturing, textiles, automotive, pharmaceuticals, and agriculture. They address trade opportunities, market dynamics, and sector-specific challenges that are pertinent to industry participants. For every commodity and industry, there are many boards, councils, and agencies.

These are just a few instances of the kinds of export-import seminars that could be helpful to exporters. Exporters must do their research and choose seminars that specifically meet their requirements, interests, and trade-related issues. Exporters should also make use of the networking possibilities provided by these seminars to establish connections with government representatives, business leaders, and other importers and exporters.

- **List of Major Exporters Meetings and Seminars in India:-**

1. India International Trade Fair (IITF, New Delhi)
2. India International Leather Fair (IILF, Chennai)
3. India International Mega Trade Fair (IIMTF, Many Locations)
4. India International Jewellery Show (IIJS, Mumbai)
5. India Electronics Week (IEW- Many Locations)
6. India International Garment Fair (IIGF, New Delhi)
7. India Wood (Bangalore International Exhibition Centre, Bengaluru)
8. India International Tea & Coffee Expo (IITCE, Kolkata)
9. India International Dairy Expo (IIDE, Mumbai)
10. India International Travel & Tourism Exhibition (IITT, Mumbai)

- **List of Major Exporters Meetings and Seminars Globally:-**

1. Canton Fair (China Import and Export Fair)
2. Gulfood (Dubai, UAE)
3. Ambiente (Frankfurt, Germany)
4. Automechanika (Various Locations Worldwide)
5. Anuga (Cologne, Germany)
6. Maison&Objet (Paris, France)
7. Arab Health (Dubai, UAE)
8. MEDICA (Düsseldorf, Germany)
9. MIPTV/MIPCOM (Cannes, France)

10. Hong Kong Electronics Fair (Hong Kong)

• • •

162

CHAPTER XV

Identifying Buyer

1) How to find and verify a Buyer?

Because of the internet and other technical advancements, it is now much easier for entrepreneurs and exporters to grow their enterprises and bring the world closer together. Finding overseas customers for export is one strategy for expanding the business, and it's much easier to do it now than it was, say, a decade ago.

Though exporting goods can be a lucrative business, there are risks associated with it, including fraud, which makes many businesses hesitant to enter the export market. Fraudulent buyers might try to cheat and scam exporters of their goods or money, which could cause them to suffer large financial losses. Exporters have to find genuine, reliable buyers minimize these risks. Exporters have to find and verify a buyer to guarantee safe and effective export transactions. Exporters may identify and validate foreign buyers by complying with specific steps and guidelines.

If you want to find potential consumers in your target markets, Exporter can carry out in-depth market research. Trade exhibitions, trade directories, business associations, and internet marketplaces are all options to find buyers for your goods. To find possible buyers, exporters can also look up trade directories, industry databases, and business directories. Seek for reliable directories that include verified businesses and contact details, specific to your industry or target markets. Exporters can also use online resources like LinkedIn and B2B marketplaces like Global Sources, TradeIndia, Alibaba, and other similar sites. Verify buyer's corporate profiles, ratings, transaction history, reputation, financial condition, and track record to confirm their reliability.

As an exporter, you can also go to international exhibitions, trade shows, and industry events that are relevant to your field of industry. Communicate with visitors, make connections with possible buyers, and get their contact details for further communications. Ask for recommendations and referrals from trade professionals, suppliers, customers, and contacts in the industry. Trustworthy source recommendations may help in confirming the reliability of you also, which will attract more buyers. Make sure that potential buyers are trustworthy by carrying out due diligence research. Acquire necessary data, including business licenses, tax identification numbers, contact details, and company registration details. Using third-party verification services or official government databases to confirm the truthfulness of this information.

Start a conversation by phone, email, or online messaging with potential buyers. To learn about their purchasing power, product specifications, business needs, and terms of payment, ask appropriate inquiries. To establish a relationship and evaluate the genuineness of their interest, have an open discussion with them. While communicating with that person. To confirm the trustworthiness and reliability of buyers, ask them for references or testimonials. Speak with their current or former business partners to find out about their opinions of the buyer's performance. Also, ask the buyer. Whenever feasible, schedule personal meetings with potential purchasers to build trust and credibility. Set up meetings at trade exhibitions, business trips, or site visits to explore business opportunities, negotiate agreements, and evaluate the buyer's competence and commitment.

To reduce the risk of payment default, give priority to secure payment options such as bank guarantees, custody offerings, and letters of credit (LC). Before completing the transaction, make sure that the terms and circumstances regarding payment have been outlined in detail and approved in writing. You can also request a 100% advance payment if the buyer is not very trustworthy, in which case you won't be taking any risks.

To assist with the process of identifying and verifying buyers, consult export support organizations, trade experts, or legal professionals. In addition to verifying the buyer on your behalf, they can offer insightful advice, help with due diligence investigations, and direction on export documentation and compliance needs. To safeguard yourself against financial issues, for instance, you can also include the Export Credit Guarantee Corporation of India (ECGC) in your agreement. It functions as a type of export insurance, and you must get in touch with them before shipping your products.

These actions, together with due diligence, help exporters find and verify buyers efficiently, reduce risks, and create enduring relationships that will benefit their export company. Never forget that there is no perfect method, therefore to make a well-informed decision, make sure to combine various approaches.

2) How to find a supplier?

For exporters who want to ensure the quality, affordability, and prompt delivery of goods for export, finding reliable vendors is essential. As an exporter, you must first specify the requirements of your buyer as well as the products you need to export, including the amount, quality standards, delivery schedule, and specifications. This will enable you to focus your search and properly convey your needs to possible suppliers. In order to identify potential vendors or suppliers in your sector or product area, conduct market research as well. To learn more about suppliers and their product offers, check out trade events, industry forums, trade groups, and internet directories. You can use directories such as supplier directories, industry databases, and business directories. Look for directories dedicated to your sector or target markets that provide certified suppliers and contact information. To find suppliers, use internet resources including sourcing platforms (like ThomasNet, and Sourcify) and B2B marketplaces like Alibaba, Global Sources, Made-in-China, Indiamart, and Trade India. To reduce the number of alternatives depending on geographical location, product type, and other factors, You can use search filters to narrow it down. You can also go to industry events, trade shows, and exhibits that are connected to your product category. Don't forget to network with exhibitors, stop by supplier booths, and get details about their offerings, specifications, and costs. You can also ask trade professionals, business associates, and contacts in the industry for recommendations and referrals. Double-check the supplier's information and Suggestions from dependable sources can assist you in identifying trustworthy suppliers with an established track record, additionally after consulting experts. You can look up information about possible suppliers on your own by visiting their websites, reading online reviews, and following them on social media. You can also look up information about the suppliers' firm history, reputation, manufacturing capacity, and certifications. Get essential information including business licenses, certifications, production capacities, and firm registration details of the buyer. Use third-party verification services or official government databases to confirm the correctness of this information.

Ask possible suppliers for sample orders so you can evaluate their product quality, consistency, and adherence to your demands before committing to a long-term agreement. Furthermore Request quotes (RFQs), along with the specifications and quantity needed for your product, should be sent to several possible suppliers. After analyzing the responses you've got, make a shortlist of suppliers who fit your requirements by comparing terms, costs, and delivery alternatives. Make sure all suppliers, product samples, quotes, and inspections are up to your standards by doing extensive testing.

Following the selection of the right supplier. Start negotiating terms and conditions, such as price, terms of payment, delivery schedule, and quality requirements, with the selected suppliers. Create and execute a written contract that details the conditions and obligations of both parties. And Develop Relationships with Them to Foster Robust Supplier Relationships Built on Open Communication, Transparency, and Trust. To create a mutually productive partnership, stay in regular communication, offer input, and swiftly address any difficulties or concerns.

Exporters may find trustworthy suppliers who satisfy their needs and help their export business succeed by following these instructions and carrying out exhaustive due diligence.

3) How to handle International Inquiries?

When a business or you as an exporter, receives an inquiry from a potential customer, sales frequently start there. The majority of sellers and exporters usually respond with a proforma invoice, sales proposal, or quote directly. Unfortunately, businesses far too frequently respond to these questions swiftly, which might cause issues later on, especially if the question relates to a possible export sale. Successful exporters make sure they respond in a way that will lead to a successful export transaction by putting internal procedures in place. And generating revenue is part of that.

You should carefully comprehend and read the contents of a sales inquiry before responding to anticipate and fulfill any requests for specific information. Verify through due diligence that the query is coming from a legitimate potential customer who can pay for your products, and find out whether it is coming from a firm or organization that is on any restricted parties lists. However, if this is your first time exporting. If possible, reply to questions within 24 to 48 hours to show that you are a professional and responsive. Prompt communication demonstrates to prospective customers your appreciation for their business and your dedication to offering top-notch customer support. Begin your response by greeting and expressing appreciation for the inquiry and thanking them for their interest in your products or services. A pleasant and friendly tone establishes a favorable tone for the discourse and invites additional participation. Make a good statement about your firm, the quality of your products and services, and your reputation as the preferred vendor/supplier to your existing clients globally. Provide thorough details on the features, specifications, cost, minimum order quantities, delivery choices, and terms of payment for your goods and services. Be honest and open when answering any possible concerns or queries up front.

Make sure that your responses are customized to each prospective buyer's unique needs, preferences, and inquiries. Customizing the communication demonstrates to them your understanding of their needs and your commitment to helping them find the ideal answer. Provide supplementary resources, if any, such as brochures, spec sheets, product catalogs, and samples. Potential customers can better grasp your goods and make educated purchasing decisions with the use of real samples and visual aids. You must give a clear explanation of your terms and conditions, including any relevant details about warranties, shipping and return policies, and other regulations. Building trust and reducing misunderstandings are achieved via communication that is clear and transparent. Make your offer in a way that will put your business in the best possible position for negotiations.

You must include all extra expenses in the quote apart from the product's price. Inland freight, air/ocean freight, handling fees, consular fees, insurance, fuel surcharge, document preparation, and other expenses are a few examples. Don't give lumpsum charges into one catch-all price category. Should you do so, you might put yourself out of business or weaken your negotiating position. After sending a quote to the buyer. Wait for feedback from them. If you don't receive any feedback. You must follow up with potential buyers to see if they have any further questions or need assistance. A polite follow-up note displays your ongoing interest and commitment to their satisfaction.

Respect the buyer's timeliness and preferences while remaining persistent in your follow-up efforts. Remain patient and consistent in your quest since a potential buyer might need several touchpoints to reach a decision. Receive input from prospective customers and apply it to enhance your offerings, customer support, and communication methods. You may better satisfy the needs and expectations of your foreign clients by utilizing the insightful information that honest feedback offers. Following these points this allows exporters to efficiently handle overseas inquiries, engage potential customers, and ultimately turn inquiries into fruitful business relationships.

4) How to Estimate and Provide a Quote?

As they give prospective customers vital information about the price and terms of buying goods or services, export estimation and issuing quotations are crucial steps in the export sales process.

Begin by collecting every relevant information required to create the export estimate and quote. This contains information on the product or service being provided, including its characteristics, quantity, cost, terms of delivery, terms of payment, and any extra fees or requirements. The costs of exporting the goods or rendering the services must be calculated by the exporter. This covers the price of manufacturing, packing, shipping, insurance, taxes, customs charges, and any other pertinent expenditures. Make sure the quote is reasonable and competitive by doing precise cost calculations.

Based on your cost calculations, the state of the market, the level of competition, and your desired profit margin decided on the export quotation's price strategy. Take into account variables like exchange rates, price fluctuations, and the pricing schemes that foreign buyers prefer.

For the buyer's consideration, prepare an expert and comprehensive export quotation document that contains all relevant information. The components including your company's information, buyer information, a description of the product or service (including features, benefits, and specifications), pricing, terms and conditions, and the quotation's validity are usually included.

Before sending the quotation, thoroughly review the export quotation document for accuracy, clarity, and completeness. Double-check all computations, terms, and conditions to avoid mistakes or misunderstandings. If necessary, get input from relevant stakeholders such as sales teams or legal consultants. Once reviewed, finalize the quotation and submit it to the buyer.

After providing the export quotation, get in touch with the customer to find out if they received it and to discuss any queries or worries they may have and follow up. Throughout the negotiating process, stay in constant contact with the buyer and show consideration for their demands.

Additionally, be ready to compromise on terms and conditions with the buyer in light of their preferences and feedback. Together with the customer, work towards a compromise that satisfies your needs as well as theirs. Proceed to formalize the contract and start the export transaction as soon as the terms are agreed upon. By following to these guidelines, exporters can provide professional, precise, and customized offers and export estimations that meet the demands of their foreign consumers, ultimately leading to successful export sales.

• • •

CHAPTER XVI

Important Websites

With the internet making the world smaller by the day, it is even easier to obtain trade data through lead generation websites and primary research sources. In this section, we will look at export business websites in India for lead generation and primary research.

1) Indian Government websites

The Indian government maintains a number of web pages and online portals devoted to promoting exports and offering guidance and assistance to exporters. You can visit this website and get all the information you need or believe will be beneficial to your company. The primary source of information for all exporters and importers doing primary searches in the export-import data bank is government data.

1. The DGFT's website

Website; www.dgft.gov.in

The DGFT is India's major regulatory authority for exports and imports. Their website includes information on export and import policies, procedures, alerts, and public notices. This website allows exporters to apply for Import-Export Codes (IECs) as well as other licenses and permissions.

2. Indian Trade Portal

Website- www.indiantradeportal.in

A single point of contact for data and services pertaining to global trade is the Indian Trade Portal. It offers information on tariffs, trade agreements, customs processes, trade regulations, and trade data. Exporters can obtain details about trade shows, market entry requirements, and export promotion initiatives.

3. The Ministry of Commerce and Industry

Website- www.commerce.gov.in

The Ministry of Commerce and Industry holds a prominent position in the development and execution of trade policies aimed at advancing exports and augmenting India's international trade. Their website provides details on projects, initiatives, and trade policies that promote exporters.

4. National Centre for Trade Information (NCTI)

Website: https://www.ncti.gov.in/

For market intelligence and trade-related information, NCTI acts as a knowledge centre. Trade databases, market research papers, trade statistics, and trade promotion activities are all accessible through their website.

5. Export Inspection Council (EIC)

Website: www.eicindia.gov.in

The export goods must be examined and certified by the Export Inspection Council of India to guarantee that quality and safety regulations are being followed. They provide information on product standards, export inspection and certification services, and legal requirements on their website.

6. Customs Department

Website: www.cbic.gov.in

The rules and processes pertaining to customs clearance are managed by the Central Board of Indirect Taxes and Customs (CBIC). On their website, you can get details on tariff classifications, duty rates, online customs clearance services, and customs procedures.

These official websites provide Indian exporters with helpful information, instructions, and assistance in navigating export procedures, gaining access to export promotion initiatives, and growing their market share abroad.These official websites provide Indian exporters with helpful information, instructions, and assistance in navigating export procedures, gaining access to export promotion initiatives, and growing their market share abroad.These official websites provide Indian exporters with helpful information, instructions, and assistance in navigating export procedures, gaining access to export promotion initiatives, and growing their market share abroad.

2) Export Promotion Councils

Export Promotion Councils (EPCs) in India are industry-specific organisations tasked with marketing and promoting exports of goods and services from India. These councils play an important role in offering aid, guidance, and support to exporters in their specific industries.

1. Federation of Indian Export Organisations (FIEO)

Website:www.fieo.org

FIEO is India's leading trade promotion organization, promoting the country's exporters and promoting foreign trade. It serves a variety of industries and offers services such as market research, trade facilitation, export marketing, and advocacy for policy.

2. Gems and Jewellery Export Promotion Council (GJEPC)

Website:www.gjepc.org

GJEPC is in charge of promoting the export of gems and jewellery from India. It represents manufacturers, importers and exporters, retailers, and other players in the gem and jewellery business. GJEPC organises trade events, buyer-seller meetings, and industry-specific training.

3. Apparel Export Promotion Council (AEPC)

Website:www.aepcindia.com

The AEPC encourages India's clothing and textile exports. It supports garment producers, exporters, and other stakeholders by organising trade shows, buyer-seller meetings, skill development programmes, and market research initiatives.

4. Shellac and Forest Products Export Promotion Council (SHEFEXIL)

Website:www.shefexil.org

SHEFEXIL promotes the export of shellac, forest/wood products, and related things from India. It helps exporters by offering market knowledge, trade promotion activities, product quality certification, and export paperwork services.

5. Cashew Export Promotion Council of India (CEPCI)

Website:www.cashewindia.org

CEPCI promotes the exports of kernels of cashew and cashew-based goods from India. It represents cashews processors, exporters, and other stakeholders, and its operations include market development, enhancement of quality, and facilitation of trade.

6. Engineering Export Promotion Council of India (EEPC India)

Website:www.eepcindia.org

EEPC India promotes exports of engineering goods, machinery, and related services from India. It helps exporters by providing market intelligence, organizing trade delegations, attending global exhibits, and conducting export-related training programs.

7. Pharmaceuticals Export Promotion Council of India (Pharmexcil)

Website:www.pharmexcil.com

Pharmexcil promotes the export of pharmaceutical products, such as medications, formulations, bulk pharmaceuticals, and medical equipment. It makes global advertising, market access, compliance with regulations, and export promotion easier for the pharma business.

By supporting exporters, providing market access, and fostering international trade, these Export Promotion Councils and a number of others encompassing other industries are essential in augmenting India's export revenues.

3) Exporters Website

India's exporters have access to several internet portals that offer useful tools, resources, and services to support global trade. India's exporters can access a number of internet portals that offer useful tools, resources, and services to support global trade. It could serve as an online business directory for exporters looking to connect with clients located outside of India. Manufacturers, suppliers, exporters, wholesalers, and providers of services across all industries can register their company on their directory in order to increase their reach both domestically and internationally. and the consumer or buyer who is trying to find your goods. This websites can offers businesses in every vertical a fantastic platform to list their goods and services and draw queries from verified buy leads, distributors, buyers, and other interested parties worldwide.

1. Alibaba India

Website: www.alibaba.com

Alibaba is a global platform for business-to-business e-commerce that links vendors and buyers globally. Alibaba India offers an avenue for Indian exporters to exhibit their merchandise and get entry to international markets.

2. Exporters India

Website:www.exportersindia.com

Exporters India is an internet network and directory for Indian exporters and manufacturers. It allows exporters to promote their products, interact with worldwide buyers, and get trade leads and commercial prospects.

3. Trade India

Website:www.tradeindia.com

Another well-known B2B platform that links Indian importers and exporters is TradeIndia. Trade leads, business directories for exporters, and online product catalogues are just a few of the many services it provides.

4. IndiaMart

Website: www.indiamart.com

One of the biggest online B2B marketplaces in India, IndiaMart links providers and buyers in a range of industries. Exporters may connect with overseas buyers, list their goods and services, and obtain business leads.

The websites of these exporters in India are important sources of information for exporters, giving them access to international markets, business prospects, trade leads, and necessary data and services to help in their export endeavours.

5) ICEGATE Overview

The Central Board of Indirect Taxes and Customs (CBIC)'s national portal for Indian Customs is called the Indian Customs Electronic Gateway (ICEGATE), and it offers electronic filing services to traders, cargo carriers, and other trading partners.

Currently, over 1.6 lakh users are registered on ICEGATE, providing services to over 12.5 lac importers and exporters. With the use of this facility, Indian Customs provides a wide range of services, such as the ability to electronically file shipping bills (an export goods declaration) and bills of entry, pay customs duties online, endorse all customs documents using a free web-based tool called Common Signer, file additional documentation online using e-Sanchit, and receive an end-to-end electronic IGST refund, among other services.

E-SANCHIT: what is it then? Customs clearance paperwork can be electronically submitted by merchants through ICEGATE's e-SANCHIT (Secure Access for Electronic Communication Harmonised Information Technology) facility. This improves efficiency in the customs clearance process by cutting down on paperwork and streamlining operations.

ICEGATE's internal links to many partner agencies, including the RBI, Banks, DGFT, DGCIS, Ministry of Steel, Directorate of Valuation, and other various authorities, enable quick Customs clearance. Online payments for taxes, customs charges, and other costs related to import and export transactions are made possible by ICEGATE. Through the website, exporters and importers can safely make payments utilising a number of different payment options, including credit/debit cards, online banking, and electronic funds transfers (EFT).

A wide range of other services are also offered by ICEGATE in addition to electronic filing, including a round-the-clock help desk for its trading partners, electronic payments for Central Excise and Service Tax, online registration for IPR, document tracking status at Customs EDI, cargo tracking, online licence verification for DEPB/DES/EPCG, IE code status, PAN-based CHA data, IGST Refund Status, and links to numerous other significant websites and resources pertaining to international trade Trade.

When everything is considered, ICEGATE is essential to the modernization of customs procedures, the advancement of digital trade, and the smooth interchange of data and electronic communications between Indian customs officials and merchants. It makes customs clearance processes more transparent, efficient, and compliant, which makes doing business easier and promotes cross-border trade.

• • •

CHAPTER XVII

Action Plan

So, after learning all the fundamentals of export business and the complex process of international trade. It's time to put it into execution and action, and you'll need to do it on your own. This chapter will help you create an action plan because if you don't have one, you'll finish this book and start from zero.

1) 200 Days Action Plan

I divided this action plan into 200 days (five months). This comprehensive 200-day action plan will walk you through the process of starting your export business systematically.

Phase 1: Research and Preparation (Day 1- 60)

During these 60 days, your primary focus will be on fundamentals such as market research, product selection, financial planning, rules and regulations, and supply chain management.

1. Market Research

- Evaluate possible export markets by considering factors including competition, limitations, and demand.
- Analyse market trends, cultural differences, and customer preferences in the targeted markets.

2. Product Selection

- Analyse products carefully, taking into account demand globally, quality, and uniqueness, to identify those that have export potential.
- Verify that the products you have chosen comply with international standards and legislation.

3. Legal and Regulatory Compliance

- Analyse and evaluate the export regulations, Taxes, and documentation needs of the targeted markets.
- During this phase, the goal and try to obtain all the required licenses, permits, and certifications for exporting as well as for exporting the specific commodity/product.

4. Financial Planning

- Determine the initial costs of production, packing, shipping, and marketing.
- Evaluate your possibilities for funding, including grants, loans, and investors.
- During this phase, avoid thinking about revenue and profits as you will also lose break-even. To stand out, concentrate on the best pricing/cost.

5. Supply Chain Management

- Find trustworthy suppliers of products or raw materials and build ties with them.
- Discuss conditions such as cost, requirements for quality, and timeframes to get product after order.

Do not rush to choose a product, apply for loans, or conclude a supplier agreement. Take each step carefully in your space. Improper product selection, applying for loans before receiving orders, and finalizing supplier agreements without evaluating their trustworthiness and punctuality can lead to future problems, including loss of reputation and money.

Phase 2: Setting Up Operations (Day 61-140)

During this phase, you have to decide how you will organize your operational activities. This includes market entry strategy, risk management, presence marketing, demonstration documentation such as a catalog, and so on.

1. Production & Supplier Optimization

- Improve production processes to meet international quality standards and increase output as required. If you are trading, request that your supplier uphold the specific standard required for you to carry on with business as regular.
- Ensure constant product quality and packaging compliance, as each country has different packaging standards and regulations for import, which the buyer will specify. However, you must be aware of the costs ahead of time because you will be targeting a certain country.

2. Logistics Planning and Set-up

- Finalise delivery methods and logistics partners, taking into account affordability and trustworthiness.
- In this case, you can think of the best freight forwarder as your logistics partner. and for customs purposes, CHA or CHB (Broker).
- Create a reliable supply chain management system to monitor shipments and inventory.

3. Market Entry Strategy

- Create an in-depth price strategy and marketing plan specific to your target markets.
- Create partnerships with regional distributors or merchants as well as both online and offline channels of distribution.

4. Create your Online Presence

- With an export-focused strategy, create or update your company website, using content in multiple languages as necessary.
- Utilise digital marketing techniques such as search engine optimization, content creation, and email marketing to increase brand recognition and draw in prospective global clientele.

5. Documentation and Compliances

- To ensure seamless export procedures, familiarise yourself with INCO terms and international trade regulations.
- Assemble the required export documents, such as packing lists, invoices, and certificates of origin.

6. Risk Management

- Determine possible risks including supply chain interruptions, political unrest, and currency volatility.
- Create backup plans to reduce risks and guarantee company operations.
- Get insurance for your company to manage risks and prevent a black day in your business (Financial Loss).

Phase 3: Market Expansion (Day 141- 200)
1. Market Vist and do fieldwork

- Participate in industry gatherings, trade shows, and exhibits to promote your goods and build commercial relationships.
- Evaluate possibilities for collaboration with local businesses, distributors, or representatives in your intended markets.

2. Customer Relationship Management

- To promote trust and commitment among overseas clients, offer excellent after-sale support and service to customers.
- To improve goods and services and raise consumer satisfaction, get opinions and testimonies.

3. Continuous Improvement

- Keep an eye on consumer preferences and market changes to adjust your offerings and strategy appropriately.

- To create innovative goods, increase productivity, and preserve competitiveness, spend money on research and development.

4. Scaling Operations

- Evaluate the scalability and production capability to satisfy the growing demand from global markets.
- To improve customer service and market penetration, consider building local offices or warehouses in strategic locations and expanding distribution networks.

By sticking to this 200-day action plan, you can build a solid basis for your export company, as successfully overcome obstacles and capitalize on possibilities for growth in overseas markets. Maintain focus, flexibility, and responsiveness to market conditions to ensure the long-term success and sustainability of any export enterprise. And now your 200 days are up, and you've launched your business and completed your foundation. From here, your sole responsibilities will be to find buyers, identify buyers, and engage in trade.

2) Links for Embassy Email, CHA, ICD & CFS List
1. CHA
To get a list of authorized CHAs, get in touch with the port or customs authorities. To find CHAs in your region, you may also look through trade association websites or online business directories about customs brokerage.

I'm providing the CHA list for the Mundra and JNPT ports here. Because these ports served as the hub for major shipping.

- JNPT CHA List Link

  https://www.jawaharcustoms.gov.in/pdf/cha-list.pdf

- Mundra Port CHA List Link

https://docs.google.com/spreadsheets/d/1Tmkwye2kChNA-cNiVGdonrYQTDEiLQE3CQLqXJ5tc4Y/edit?usp=sharing

2. Embassy

Go to the embassy or consulate of your target nation's official website. Email addresses are usually available in the "Contact Us" or "Consular Services" sections of most embassies.

As an alternative, you might use government websites or internet directories that include the addresses of embassies and consulates around the globe.

Some Major Embassy Email IDs of Economics and Commercial are as follows:-

1. Germany:- com.berlin.mea.gov.in
2. Poland:- comwing.warsaw@mea.gov.in
3. China:- cons.beijing@mea.gov.in & cons1.beijing@mea.gov.in
4. UAE:- fscom.kl@mea.gov.in & fsca.abudhabi@mea.gov.in
5. UK:-inf.london@mea.gov.in & inf.london@mea.gov.in
6. USA:- usa-fscom.klamea.gov.in, USA-fscom.kl@mea.gov.in & Com3.washington@mea.gov.in
7. Australia:- com.canberra@mea.gov.in, canberra@meg.gov & com.canberra@mea.gov.in
8. Netherlands:- trade.thehague@mea.gov.in
9. Chile:- com1.santiago@mea.gov.in
10. Saudhi Arabia:- ccom.riyadh@mea.gov.in
11. Russia:- eco.moscow@mea.gov.in & eco1.moscow@mea.gov.in
12. Thailand:- Bankok@mea.gov.in

Similarly, you can look up all of the contact information, including email addresses, for the specific nation you are trying to reach in an online government directory for later use.

3. Exhibitions and Trade shows

Of course! Participating in exhibits and trade shows may be a great way to present your goods, make connections with possible partners and customers, and keep up with market developments. You may get a list of all the trade shows happening in the current year, along with information about booking options, dates, and times, as well as the organizers, by clicking on the provided link. Trade exhibitions for all sectors and industries can be found here.

https://www.eventseye.com/fairs/st1_trade-shows_international-fairs.html

3. ICD and CFS

For a list of ICDs and CFSs in your area, check with the port or customs authority in your community.

To find ICDs and CFSs close to your location or target markets, use online tools including industry associations, shipping company websites, and logistics directories.

https://commerce.gov.in/wp-content/uploads/2020/03/MOC_636517146051928242_List_ICDs_CFSs_AFSs_01-01-2018-2.pdf

• • •

Images

Container Lifting Crane

Chilli Ready for Export, Stuffed in Reefer Container

JNPA, Nhava Sheva, Navi Mumbai

MSC AZRA on Board at Terminal-1 JNPT Port

Pilot Boat at Port

New Port- Vadhvan Port

Forklift

Container Racked one-on-one at CFS

Details Printed on Containers

Pomegranate Packing and Ready for Export

Special Equipment on Flat Rack and Ready for Export

Major Ports and ICDs in India

Rank	Company name	TEUs	Fleet capacity	Location
1	MSC (Mediterranean Shipping Company)	5.3 million	783	Switzerland/Italy
2	Maersk	4.1 million	687	Denmark
3	CMA CGM Group	3.5 million	628	France
4	COSCO Shipping Lines	2.9 million	475	China
5	Hapag-Lloyd	1.8 million	257	Germany
6	Evergreen Marine Line	1.69 million	215	Taiwan
7	ONE (Ocean Network Express)	1.68 million	219	Japan
8	HMM Co Ltd	800 thousand+	71	South Korea
9	Yang Ming Marine Transport Corp	700 thousand+	93	Taiwan
10	ZIM Integrated Shipping Service Ltd	500 thousand+	129	Israel

Top 10 Shipping Containers Companies

Epilogue

As we wrap up our vessel journey through the complicated landscape of export business, it's critical to reflect on the lessons gained and the paths ahead. This book has covered many aspects of international trade, including market research and product adaptation, as well as logistics and legal considerations. We've explored the challenges and opportunities that come with going outside national borders, providing insights and success tactics.

Understand that adaptability and foresight are critical in the ever-changing world of export business. Markets adapt, legislation changes and geopolitical landscapes move around. Despite this uncertainty, there is enormous opportunity for growth and innovation. The global marketplace is enormous, allowing firms of various sizes and industries to achieve success.

As exporters, we must welcome change and see it as a possibility and opportunity to grow. To stay ahead of the competition, we must constantly refine our planning and strategies by relying on technology, data, and collaboration. Collaboration and knowledge sharing are crucial because we can benefit from one another's experiences and insights, just like I am sharing my experience and knowledge. And don't give up on hope during the process of progress; one day you'll be successful.

We also need to keep in mind how our efforts will affect society as a whole. Export business is about more than just making money; it's about building relationships, promoting understanding, and advancing society and our economy. We can add value to our businesses and the communities and places we operate in by adopting sustainability, inclusion, and ethical practices.

Let us, as we finish this book, start our export adventures with newfound vigor and purpose. Let's face the obstacles head-on, resilient and optimistic, understanding that every setback is also a hidden opportunity. And let's not forget that, in the end, the real test of success is not just how much money we make, but also how much good we provide for the country and world.

May all of your endeavors prove successful, your contributions persistent, and your enterprises profitable. And let's rank India #1 in terms of exports.

Cheers to you all, exporters, and may the winds of opportunity always flow in your direction.

-Vedant Borle

• • •

Acknowledgements

I would like to express my gratitude to the following people and institutions:

To my mom and dad, Archana Borle and Sudhakar Borle, for their constant support during the ups and downs.

To my friend Mayank Choudhary, for giving me the thought of writing a book.

To my friend Samruddhi Gore, who encouraged me and made me explore new things.

My institution, NMIMS University, opened my doors to the corporate world and taught me how to think from a 360-degree perspective.

To my managers, Swapna Singh, Thubel Thomas, Sarath Chandran, Suresh Anand, Dr. Edna Ayme-Yahil, Bhaskar Priyadarshi, Atirek Aanand, and my friends & colleagues at Cogoport Pvt Ltd.

To my friend and colleague Raghav Sand at Cogoport Pvt Ltd, who has helped me with the book starting and has given me advice on how to structure and frame it.

To the Maharashtra Warehousing Corporation and Jawaharlal Nehru Port Authority (JNPA) for granting permission to visit the JNPT/Nhava Sheva port to understand the field operations at the port and CFS.

To my clients, exporters, and overseas partners from all over the world for sharing their knowledge.

To the Saurabh Bothra & HaBuild Community, I could not have written this book and worked day and night without your tips on good physical health, mental clarity, and energy.

And to Bhargava Adepalley, Yamini Shekhar, Selva Priya, and Nidha Haris of Notion Press, who never stop reminding me to finish the book and provide constant support.

Image Credits

1. 20 Ft Standard Container image © Indiamart.com
2. 40Ft Standard Dry Container image © Alibaba.com
3. 40Ft High Cube Container image © Shipping Container House Plans
4. 20FT Open Top Container image © Marine Traffic.com
5. 40FT Open Top Container image © Aajjo.com
6. 20FT Flat Rack Container image © Lotus Containers.com
7. 40FT Flat Rack Container image © Lotus Containers.com
8. 20FT Reefer Container image © Alibaba.com
9. 40FT Reefer Container image © Mobilemodularcontainers.com
10. 20FT ISO Tank Container image © Tradecorpshippingcontainers.com
11. 40FT ISO Tank Container © Multitanks.es
12. Incoterms Chart © Exportmarkters.ca
13. Use of Incoterm: For Transfer of Risk © erd.export-u.com
14. Format of Proforma Invoice © Inpaspages.com
15. Format of Commercial Invoice © docshipper.com
16. Format of Packing List © Issuu.com
17. Format of Certificate of Origin © Pinterest.com
18. Format of Bill of Lading © Formspal.com
19. Format of Bill of Exchange © Mybillbook.com
20. ICD and Ports Map © Lotus Containers.com

*Please contact us if you have any feedback on the
book or need assistance. You can reach us by email
at fromlocaltoglobal.consultant@gmail.com.*